crazy
CYCLING CHICK
The Inspirational Journey of
Angie Across America

Angeline Tan

Marshall Cavendish
Editions

© 2016 Angeline Tan

Images courtesy of Angeline Tan
Design: Lynn Chin

Published by Marshall Cavendish Editions
An imprint of Marshall Cavendish International
1 New Industrial Road, Singapore 536196

Other Marshall Cavendish Offices:
Marshall Cavendish Corporation. 99 White Plains Road, Tarrytown NY 10591-9001, USA • Marshall Cavendish International (Thailand) Co Ltd. 253 Asoke, 12th Flr, Sukhumvit 21 Road, Klongtoey Nua, Wattana, Bangkok 10110, Thailand • Marshall Cavendish (Malaysia) Sdn Bhd, Times Subang, Lot 46, Subang Hi-Tech Industrial Park, Batu Tiga, 40000 Shah Alam, Selangor Darul Ehsan, Malaysia

Marshall Cavendish is a trademark of Times Publishing Limited.

National Library Board, Singapore Cataloguing in Publication Data
Name(s): Tan, Angeline.
Title: Crazy cycling chick : the inspirational journey of Angie across America / Angeline Tan.
Other title(s): Inspirational journey of Angie across America
Description: Singapore : Marshall Cavendish Editions, [2016]
Identifier(s): OCN 952163039 | ISBN 978-981-47-7114-6 (paperback)
Subject(s): LCSH: Cycling--United States. | Bicycle touring--United States. | Women cyclists--Malaysia.
Classification: DDC 796.60973--dc23

Printed in Singapore by JCS Digital Solutions Pte Ltd

To Jason, my husband, partner, supporter,
mentor, encourager and confidant – I thank God each and
every day for the incredible gift He's given me in you.
Thank you for showing me how to live and love.

Contents

Astoria, OR
Tillamook, OR
Coburg, OR
Baker City, OR
Missoula, MT
West Yellowstone, MT
Jackson, WY
Rawlins, WY
Newton, KS
Pueblo, CO

"All I had was a game plan: pedal 100 miles or more each day, stay in a different town each night until I got to the other side of the country."

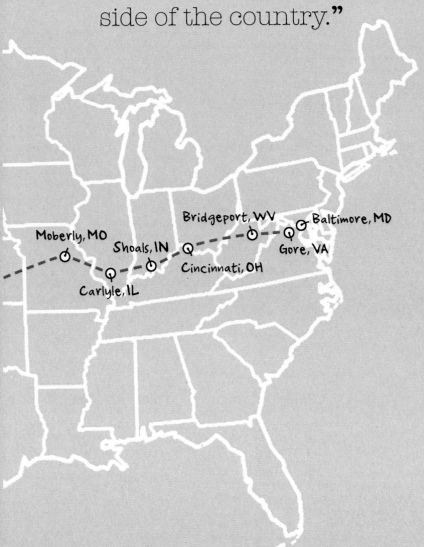

Moberly, MO

Shoals, IN

Carlyle, IL

Bridgeport, WV

Baltimore, MD

Cincinnati, OH

Gore, VA

Introduction

The days and months following my bicycle ride across the United States, I was often asked what inspired me to do it, how the adventure felt, what I saw and experienced, who I met, what I ate, what the challenges I faced on the road were.

But more often, I'd be met with expressions of, "You what?" or "No way!" or "You're kidding ..." and when they realized I wasn't, they'd say, "Wow, that's very impressive. Really impressive. Wow." And they'd be silent for a little while, as if to wrap their heads around the idea before asking more questions about cycling across a continent.

In between those awkward moments of silence, I'd squirm a little because the truth was, I didn't think that what I did was extraordinary. All I had was a game plan: pedal 100 miles or more each day, stay in a different town each night until I got to the other side of the country, heave a sigh of relief, and declare to myself, "There, you did it. You rode across America."

While I certainly felt stronger mentally, like I had been forged into indestructible steel after being riddled with very

◀ Railroad tracks along the coast at Nehalem Bay State Park in Oregon.

harsh weather and a host of physical and mental challenges associated with a multiple-week bike ride, I felt no differently about my personal identity. In my heart and mind, I was still the same ol' Angie. I didn't feel superhuman or that I was a super endurance cyclist like Mike Hall or Juliana Buhring who circumnavigated the globe (18,000 miles) on their bicycles in 92 and 152 days respectively.

Following the earlier exclamations of "Wow!" or "Oh my gosh, you did what?", there would often be two groups of people asking different sets of questions.

Firstly, the athletic ones, you know, the cyclists, runners, hikers, gym-goers, Cross-fitters. They'd ask technical questions concerning the ride: "How did you plan your route?", "What did you eat?" and "How did you fill up on water?"

The second group, usually the non-athletes, would be more baffled than the first group, and they'd ask more fundamental questions like, "Why would you do something like that?", "What inspired you to ride your bike across the country?", "Why didn't you drive instead?" and "Did you do it to raise funds or create awareness for something?"

Both sets of questions are valid, and in the pages that follow, I have attempted to answer as many of them as I can.

More importantly, the primary motivation for this book is to share as honestly as possible, the journey of a dream from conception to reality.

Growing up as a highly-driven and ·motivated child, I often saw men and women accomplishing great successes or feats and thought to myself, wow, that's incredible. I want to be like that.

What I didn't realize then as a child, and what I now know as an adult, having personally met and spoken to people with considerable achievements in their lives, is that behind their accomplishments was a huge amount of hard work. Behind the scenes, away from the public eye and spotlight, is a journey riddled with doubt, discouragement, and disappointment, topped with incredible amounts of sweat and grit, pain and conflict, determination and perseverance.

I want my journey to be an open book, where I candidly lay out my struggles in the pursuit of my dream to cycle across America. This is my story.

Author's Note:

Throughout this book there are mentions of 39 and 40 days. While my goal was to cross the country in 40 days, I eventually did it in 39.

"Men who go looking for the source of a river are merely looking for the source of something missing in themselves, and never finding it."

– Sir Richard Burton on the mental state of the explorer

Prologue

I was flat on my back. The tears ran, hot and salty, down the sides of my face into my ears but I didn't care. I could not lift myself up at all. I could not even muster an ounce of strength to sit up. I hurt everywhere ... and my tire was flat. Again. I didn't know if I was going to make it. I just wanted to curl into a ball and give up. Call home and maybe get my husband to send an emergency helicopter to airlift me home to sunny California, away from the summer snow, the mosquitoes and endless miles of nothingness. What was I doing, racing across America?

I looked at Derek's face and saw the same, desperate empty hopelessness I felt in my soul. That was it. We were done.

But we still had 1,800 miles to go ...

Could I live with myself if I quit now?

The pain in my limbs would go, the ache in my chest would heal, but would the torture of quitting haunt me the rest of my life?

Was this really the end of myself I had reached, or just a version of the infamous "wall" that athletes hit?

▲ Derek and I at Stites, Idaho.

Here We Go!

Derek Wilson

"So, you wanna ride together?" I asked enthusiastically.

"Yeah, sure. I'll like to. I mean, I think it'll be fun to do that," Derek responded, trying to match my enthusiasm. I would later discover that he is an overall nice, accommodating and always agreeable fella.

"Yeah, I'm thinking it's gonna be such a long journey, it'll be great to have someone to talk to. Beats riding alone, don't you think?"

"Yea, definitely ..." And then a silence that lingered a tad too long.

"So, you think we're gonna get along well and not kill each other on the road?" He laughed nervously. Poor guy, what was I expecting him to say? Laughing was the best he could do to thwart the awkwardness.

That was one of two conversations I had with Derek Wilson, a stranger who promised to ride with me cross-country. We would keep each other safe on the road.

I met him for the first time a day before we were to set off on the longest ride of our lives. I had seen pictures of him on Facebook and knew what he looked like. Long hair, bushy beard, always in cycling clothes, posing gleefully with other cyclists. I thought he looked like a very happy hipster on two wheels.

We had planned to meet in the historic fishing town of Astoria in Oregon on June 6, 2015, the starting point of the Trans America Bike Race (details of this race to follow in a later chapter).

That afternoon, after having settled into a handsome boutique hostel together with other racers of the Trans America Bike Race, I explored the quaint little town with my husband, Jason.

Coming out of a bookstore, I saw a young man in a crumpled T-shirt, shorts, and flip flops, pushing an old, worn bike. I recognized him from across the street, and gestured to Jason beside me, "Look, that's him. Derek."

In person, his beard looked larger and bushier and his hair longer and messier than his pictures portrayed. There were several small holes in his white T-shirt.

We exchanged courtesies, like two people meeting for the first time, except it wasn't the first time; we'd spoken on the phone twice and exchanged several emails while we were hammering out the logistics of the ride. He spoke with a certain drawl, like some Midwesterners. I later found out he's from Kansas.

It was awkward because here we were, meeting for the first time, and from the next day on, we were expecting to be best friends for the next six weeks. It was a case of intentional friendship – the situation required that we become friends, and not just ordinary friends, but fast friends, because we would be counting on each other to survive the next six weeks together.

As we spoke, I studied his bike – an old, 1984 Schwinn. Its frame was a pale blue, like the color of a cloudless sky, except it was duller, because it was matte, and not the soft and serene blue you see in the sky. A metal rack perched precariously on the front of the bike. On it rested a black burlap sack full of what looked like clothes. Protruding from the sides of the rear was another bike rack with pannier bags on each side.

His bags and metal racks looked heavy, bulky, and uncooperative for cycling uphill. I was doubtful if we would achieve a comfortable pace cycling together, with him lugging all that extra weight. He didn't even look muscular.

I had my doubts but managed to crack a joke. "So Derek, are you ready to be my best friend for the next 40 days?"

He laughed a dry laugh. "Yeah ... I think so." I would later be accustomed to his long drawn "yeahs" which carried an air of uncertainty about them, the kind of yeah you'd hear prefacing an "I don't know."

And so here I was, on the verge of taking off for several weeks with a man I had just met, who looked, smelled and spoke like a Bohemian, and Jason did not betray a single misgiving, although he too had his doubts if Derek would be able to ride with all that extra weight. Derek would later mail his bags home.

The Idea

How did this crazy cross-country idea come about? Well, this takes us back to July 2013.

I had just completed an Ironman distance triathlon in Northern California. As many athletes would agree, the day after a hard race is when you slump back into reality. I found myself lolling about at home aimlessly. The high and adrenaline of the race had worn off. All that was left was an empty void and I ached on the inside. It's the kind of feeling you have when you've just taken the wildest roller coaster ride of your life, which terrified you beyond your greatest fears, and after you have sat through it like an adult, no doubt screaming your lungs out in the process, you step off the platform and think, "Whoa, that was insane. I'm never doing that again," and seconds later, as if struck by momentary memory loss, you say, "What's next?"

It was in this vulnerable state of mind that I found myself doodling, I mean, Googling, for something meaningful. Something more than the Ironman. What could possibly fill that void after a race that consisted of a 2.4-mile swim, 112-mile bike ride and a 26.2-mile run? It would have to be something significantly longer, harder, and more extreme.

And then it came. Like a flash of lightning it came and went. A thought. A crazy thought.

As if to justify the absurdity of that idea, I jumped on Google Maps for verification.

As clear to me now as it was then, I saw this:

San Francisco to New York City: 3,000 miles by car.

I smiled.

I would cycle across America.

||||||||||||||||

I would later realize that 3,000 miles by car didn't translate to the same distance on bicycle. Bicycles are not permitted on major freeways, and typically travel on longer routes that weave through backroads and mountain passes. There are also different routes and distances to cross the country, most commonly the northern, central or southern routes which range from 2,500 to 4,400 miles.

I would eventually complete the Northwestern-central 4,000-mile route, at a pace of 100 miles a day.

Finding Coach Colin

Cycle 4,000 miles in under 40 days. How would I train myself to do that? It was a daunting goal and it baffled my little brain.

In desperation, I turned to Twitter. I asked a simple question in 140 characters. Miraculously, a British ultra distance adventure cyclist picked up my question and suggested that I check with her coach, Colin. She didn't say much, but I was immediately sold. She was an ultra distance cyclist; I was learning to be one. She said Colin was amazing, nice and patient. As a rookie, I needed just such a coach. And if he could transform her into the ultra distance cyclist that she was, then perhaps he could do the same with me.

The power of recommendation. It never gets old, and it sure is effective.

Each year, Colin trains 12 athletes, two of whom at no charge. When I reached out to Colin, I didn't have money to pay for his coaching services. Fortunately for me, he had one more slot for an unpaid athlete.

Power of the Human Body

On the surface, it sounded easy. In order to ride 100 miles a day in eight hours, I would have to train myself to ride eight hours daily, correct? No. That would require way too many hours of training for several months in a row. I wouldn't have a life apart from cycling. Besides, I might burn myself out before reaching the starting line.

Coach Colin had me ride for just two hours a day, four times a week, and two back-to-back days (typically on the weekends) where I would ride six to eight hours each day.

I wasn't always a good student. I would cut corners and try to ride as little as I could, especially on the back-to-back days. I struggled with motivation and discouragement but he never lost his patience with me. He never stopped believing in me and always knew the right, gentle thing to say to get me back on my bike again.

I learned that the key was consistency, not volume, speed, force, or strength. Training was simply hour after hour of saddle time and consistent pedaling. Endurance was about developing a rhythm, a comfortable pace, and settling into a routine that lasted for hours in a low heart rate zone.

Shorter rides on the weekdays helped me develop pedal-stroke consistency while longer back-to-back rides simulated a typical day's ride. It amazes me how just two days a week could get my body ready for a 39-day ride.

I began to appreciate the intricacy of the human body as I observed changes in mine over six months of training – my body was able to take little adjustments, imprint them onto my muscles and mind, and those little imprints, over time, built my overall endurance fitness. While I had been training consistently for short durations, those replicated efforts helped me improve over longer durations and distances.

This, essentially, is what muscle memory is – imprinting a kinetic task into memory through repetition.

And this also made me realize that there are no shortcuts. Success requires a daily, consistent chipping along the path to your goal. Superhumans are really people with extreme discipline, diligence, and focus.

▲ View of Snake River, which flows
between and separates northeast
Oregon from Idaho.

Oregon

day 4 Encounter: Jeff Venable

Sweat dripped down my forehead. The cool morning air was replaced by steadily rising temperatures. Or was it my body temperature rising as I ground my way up a mountain pass?

Leaving Prineville for Mitchell, the Ochoco Highway was long and quiet. Cars were few and spread out. Two thirds of the 47 miles was uphill.

In a state of semi-stupor, suddenly, my eyes lit up. I had spotted a colorful object moving in a faraway distance. It was approaching Derek and me from the opposite direction. I couldn't quite make out what it was but noticed that it was traveling very, very slowly.

As the gap between us narrowed, it appeared to be a man on foot. What was a man doing in the middle of summer along a long highway?

Dressed like a cyclist in a bright jersey and thigh-length lycra shorts, he was actually a runner. An American flag stuck out from a lightweight daypack strapped to his shoulders. Everything on him was screaming colors and it cheered Derek and me up. Bright colors always did that.

View of Sumpter Valley in Oregon.

A longtime runner and retired firefighter, Jeff Venable had decided to raise funds for firefighters injured in the line of duty, and to fulfill a childhood dream of running across America. How long was he planning to complete his 3,600-mile journey? 102 days. He would run up to 35 miles each day. Gulp.

As we parted ways, we wished him well and I thought, here was a resolute man. In the coming days, when my ride got tough and my butt and legs hurt, I would think of Jeff putting one foot in front of the other until he reached New York.

When my motivation waned, I would recall the bright colors of a man running across America and smile.

 – – – – – – – – – – – – – – –

WHAT IF

Growing up in a frugal household in Malaysia with an extremely strict father, I lived in constant fear.

I feared my father flying off the hooks and caning me in his anger. I feared my school grades did not match up to his expectations of me.

One day when I was twelve, after I had been whipped several times with a cane, as blood oozed out of the tender, split skin on my buttocks, I shut the door to my bedroom, dropped to my knees, raised my clenched fists to heaven, and declared, "Someday, I will get out of this misery. I will not be intimidated by my father. I will escape this pain and do something remarkable in my life."

The idea for cycling across America, a project I have coined Angie Across America so that it is catchy and easy to remember (think triple A), wasn't simply birthed in 2014 – it was a dream that was many years in the making, one which sprouted out of that inner resolution I had made when I was twelve.

Of course I didn't know then that I would ride across America. I just knew that someday I would do something that pushed myself to the extreme; something big; something I would be proud of.

Fast forward over twenty years later, when I conceived the idea for Angie Across America, I decided that it would be a dream I would relentlessly pursue and accomplish, despite my fears.

Will I be able to complete the journey?
Will I be able to raise the funds I need?
Will I be in danger?
Will there be racism?
Will I meet rough characters?

Fear is paralyzing. Like a thick fog that blurs the vision, it creates an illusion that the path ahead is more dangerous and risky than it really is. Fear concocts excuses and stops one from moving forward.

I learned that the only way to overcome fear is to practice what sporting giant Nike proclaims in its famous marketing slogan: *Just Do It.*

So I faced my fear head-on. And when I did, it was liberating! My internal language started to change. I found myself asking:

What if I can't fail?

▲ Lolo Pass, which marks my
crossing the state line from Idaho
into Montana.

Idaho

day 7 Salmon River

Sodding, pouring rain.

Riding next to the rapidly flowing Salmon River, it felt like Mother Nature had just tipped the river over and emptied its contents onto us, a bucketful at a time.

The Salmon River runs through 425 miles of some of the most rugged and isolated terrain in the continental United States, with canyons deeper than those of the Grand Canyon. It is the longest free-flowing river in the lower 48 states, without a dam on its main stem. Nicknamed The River of No Return, it used to accommodate one-way traffic in the 1900s when equipment for miners and homesteaders was loaded on big, flat-bottomed boats bound for Riggins. At the end of the journey, the boats would be torn apart to be sold as lumber as they couldn't make their way back up the river, given the steep rapids.

We rode for more than two hours through that downpour, clothes soaked through, teeth chattering, bodies shaking with cold, until we finally came to Riggins, a small town where the main Salmon River meets the Little Salmon River.

A popular weekend spot for salmon fishing and outdoor adventures like kayaking and white water rafting, every room in Riggins' five motels was taken.

In dire need of shelter from the rain and cold, we ignored the "No Vacancy" signs and enquired from motel to motel. When we reached the last motel, its phone rang, the motel owner picked it up, and to our joy, it was a customer calling to cancel his reservation. We had a room!

We were promptly welcomed with small cups of Indonesian tea, home brewed by the American owner's Indonesian wife. The couple also runs a take-out food stall in the courtyard, to which we immediately scurried and placed our order for home cooked Indonesian-Chinese food. Ah, the warm and familiar taste of home, in a faraway white American town in Idaho, of all places!

After dinner, we fell asleep to the loud sounds of the rushing Salmon River.

day 9 Lolo Pass

My body protested vehemently – everything hurt. My legs felt like lead, my saddle bone was riddled with pain, my breathing was sorely labored, my face frozen with the cold. Raindrops were starting to solidify. I spotted snow piling up on the sides of the road. I couldn't stop often or for long because the cold would grip me. I whispered silently to myself, three miles to go. Fact was, I had twelve painful miles ahead to reach the summit. It seemed, however, that climbing three miles at a time was all I could handle. In despairing moments, breaking a monumental task into little installments was the best way to move forward.

I had ridden over 800 miles in the past eight days. Each day consisted of eight to ten hours of pure, brute cycling, mostly uphill. I climbed an average of 5,000 feet (1,524 meters) each day, equivalent to climbing the 102-story Empire State Building four times. While most office workers sit on comfortable cushioned chairs for eight hours, I sat on a hard, stiff saddle and pedaled for the same number of hours, if not more.

Today was no different. By midday, I had been pedaling uphill for six hours and 65 miles. To say the least, I was exhausted. All I could focus on was the destination ahead: Lolo Pass. The summit brings with it a tempting promise: crossing the state line to Montana. While the ride had been tormenting on many levels, the prospect of crossing state lines kept me motivated.

The last 12 miles to the summit were the hardest. I pushed with every last ounce of energy to the summit, heaved a sigh of relief, and cried. I had nothing left in me. No strength, will, or spirit left. I felt soulless.

Hells Canyon, a ten-mile wide canyon bordering the states of Oregon and Idaho.

EARLY YEARS

Malaysia. 1978 – 1995

I was born in Johor Bahru, a mid-size town on the southernmost tip of Peninsular Malaysia. The town was up-and-coming in 1978, the year I was born, and has since grown into a city clamoring with immigrants from the northern parts of the peninsular working in various industries like construction, retail, and food and beverage. Johor Bahru's economy grew, in large part, thanks to neighboring Singapore's booming economic growth.

Separated by a waterway less than a mile wide, Singapore grew from a newly independent country in 1965 with third-world infrastructure and limited capital to become one of the most prosperous nations in the world today. All of this success is carried on a land mass of a mere 276 square miles, which is half the size of Los Angeles (502 square miles), or two thirds the size of New York City (468 square miles).

I was born into a lower middle class family to parents who held the humble vocations of teaching and nursing. Despite their lack of financial means, my dad saw to it that my siblings and I received the best education that he and my mom could afford. He read widely several hours a day, poring through the local newspaper, magazines, and books about current affairs and economics. I must have inherited his thirst for learning because I read voraciously as a child, devouring any book my dad would purchase used from my older cousins. I read several books at a time, finishing them within a week. It always made my dad smile when he'd peek into my room to see me lying in bed, reading, gripping the final pages of the book gingerly, eager to conclude the tale, but reluctant for the journey to end.

The quest for knowledge also meant asking lots of questions. In fact, the more I asked, the happier my father was. When I didn't ask a question, he'd probe, "Why didn't you ask?" I'd shrug, and come up with one to appease him. That would get him talking more. I am grateful that he instilled in me a depth for curiosity and inquisitiveness that extends to this day.

And perhaps, it is this sense of wonder that made me, an Asian transplant, want to discover America and all its beauty.

DRIVEN TO ATHLETICISM
Singapore. 2008.

I was in my mid-twenties, in the prime of my life, and deeply unhappy. I held a dead-end, desk-bound job in a law firm, forlornly watching the world pass me by while I checked in from Monday to Friday, 9:00 a.m. to 6:00 p.m., without aspirations or activities to get excited about. I was barely working out, save for several short swims a week, gradually gaining weight and feeling lethargic all the time.

One morning, as I sat in the bathroom trying to wake myself up for another day of work, I thought, I feel tired all day even with eight hours of sleep each night. Heck, I could do with an hour less of sleep and pack in a run to start my morning instead.

The next morning I got up at 5:00 a.m., fresh and excited. I had roped in my husband as my running partner. Together we headed out in the dark. We plodded along slowly at first, as we struggled to find our running legs. After twenty minutes, in between big gasps for air, he slowed down to a walking pace and sheepishly announced that he was turning around and heading home, while waving his hand to signal that I should carry on running. I did, and felt stronger with each step. An hour later, I got home and checked Google Maps for the distance I ran. I was astonished! Not only had I outrun my husband, I'd completed six miles – not bad for someone who had been physically inactive for a decade since high school! Encouraged, I woke up at 5:00 a.m. again the next morning. My husband pulled the sheets over his head, pleaded with me to let him sleep, and asked that I run without him.

"But, how will I keep safe? It's dark outside," I tried to persuade him.

"You'll be fine. You did fine yesterday by yourself, didn't you?"

I relented, laced up, and headed into the dark by myself. Taking a big breath, I ran.

And ran. An hour each day. Six miles each time. Rain or shine. Dark or otherwise. I started eating better. I didn't even have to try. It came naturally as a result of running. I had little desire for sweets and started reducing sugar in my tea and coffee.

Several months later, I cut sugar entirely from my tea and coffee.

Little by little, I noticed my weight go down. My arms were more toned, my waist got narrower.

In six months, I lost 20 pounds from running and eating better.

FROM ASIA TO AMERICA

Singapore. 1996 – 2011

I had jobs as a paralegal to an audio editor, a television production house researcher, and eventually a real-estate agent, but I wasn't finding my niche. My husband, whom I had met and married in Singapore, was a civil engineer graduate who taught himself computer programming. He was drawn to Silicon Valley which practically glitters with all things technology and entrepreneurship. When he proposed moving to California, I was absolutely delighted and said yes without thinking twice. I saw it as an opportunity to begin fresh, and perhaps, rediscover my purpose in life.

California. Spring 2012.

I was like a caged animal let loose into the wild. The outdoors became my playground. I found a local cycling club that rode every day of the week, and jumped on the bandwagon to explore the land. My bike rides would soon reveal how beautiful California is: mountain ranges dot the landscape with their swollen, majestic contours, clothed in colors of green in the spring and fall, and golden brown in summer; deep valleys filled with overgrown thickets; looming redwood trees rise to astounding heights of over 300 feet; and expansive reservoirs and lakes reflect the often cloudless blue sky.

Its Mediterranean climate makes cycling all the more enjoyable. Being close to the ocean, the temperature is usually moderated — winters are warmer and summers are cooler.

Till today I pinch myself daily for living in one of the most beautiful places on earth.

Sometimes I'd bring my husband, who is not a cyclist, to see the same views. We'd drive to a mountain summit along the coast, and surveying the horizon, I'd remark to him, "Isn't it beautiful?" He'd nod and agree. But I could tell that he didn't "savor" the views as deeply as I did on my bike. That which you work for always tastes sweeter; the rewards more precious. This, I discovered, is what it means by the "sweetness of labor". Nobel laureate American author Ernest Hemingway puts it best: "It is by riding a bicycle that you learn the contours of a country best, since you have to sweat up the hills and coast down them."

If California was so beautiful, I thought, surely the rest of America must be stunning as well! I wanted to see all of it. Here I was, living in America. This would be the most opportune time for me to travel across the country. But I didn't want to get in a car, travel several hundred miles, stop for scenic views, gas, food and restroom breaks, drive some more, and find a hotel to stay the night in. I wanted to work for the sights and power myself across the country, even if that meant a slower and longer journey.

Road to Dubois, Wyoming, ▶
home to a significant group
of creatives including writers,
artists, photographers, musicians
and songwriters, presumably
drawn to the remote town by its
relatively moderate climate
and remarkable scenery.

▲ Riding into the tiny town
of Wisdom, Montana, with the
Bitterroot mountain range in
the background.

Montana

day 10 Chief Joseph Pass

I couldn't feel anything. Every body part was frozen through. My hands were numb. My feet were rigid and stone-hard. Even my heart felt like a cold lump in my chest.

It was dark and wet when we rolled into the tiny town of Wisdom, Montana at half past nine. Not a single soul was out in the streets. Relying on dim street lights, we made our way to the one of only two motels in town, the Nez Perce, located at the far edge of the tiny town.

I was still shaking uncontrollably when I checked in. I sat down on the edge of the bed, not caring that I was dirtying the clean sheets with my soaked clothes, and reflected on the misery of the day.

It had started relatively overcast. We rode in strong winds with dark clouds looming behind the mountains. I was hoping we would not ride into a storm but every pedal closer to the mountain indicated that we would.

We sought shelter in convenience stores along the way. In Sula, we stopped to warm ourselves in a convenience store by the side of the road. There was a campground on site, and we debated cutting the day short, having only ridden 74 miles. But we had a target to meet. If we slacked even for a day, we would have lots of catching up to do.

We decided to bite the bullet and keep riding. The climb to Chief Joseph Pass was arduous. The air got thinner, the winds chillier, and our legs grew terribly weary. I often wondered if the cars zooming past us would stop to offer some sympathy, because we looked like we needed it. It was written all over our faces. Perhaps the drivers couldn't see our faces. They were obscured by snow, rain, and helmets. It was miserable to be out driving, much less cycling, in such weather. I imagined the drivers thinking what a bunch of crazies we were to cycle in such conditions.

Occasionally we would stop to eat an apple to refuel our draining energy, but the winds got so chilly we only took a bite or two, and had to resume pedaling.

When we finally arrived at the steep, snowy summit of Chief Joseph Pass, I cried. I wasn't sure if I did because I was relieved or because the journey had taken everything out of me. Crying was a final expression.

The worst wasn't over. There was no place to stay the night. The next town was 28 miles away. By that point, I was so utterly drained of energy and willpower, I would have crouched in the snow and sobbed and refused to carry on if not for Derek's encouragement to keep pedaling to warm my body up.

We flew downhill on our bikes for ten miserably cold miles on slippery wet roads before pedaling the remaining 18 miles to Wisdom. I was convinced I had never experienced a more extreme situation than in that moment. I could not feel my hands on the handlebar, much less clutch my brakes. I was concerned I would slip and die. Thoughts of my husband, family and friends flashed through my mind.

Day Ten. Would my journey across America end here?

Trans America Bike Race

I knew I wanted to cycle across America, but I wasn't sure how to develop a road map to get there, so I consumed cycling in all manner and form – movies and documentaries, blogs and websites, races and adventures.

I read about the Race Across America, reputed to be the toughest bicycle race on earth, where solo racers pedal up to 22 hours and nap no more than two hours a day to pedal 3,000 miles in under 12 days. People who attempt the Race Across America are often dubbed superhuman.

I couldn't imagine riding my bicycle for that many hours each day. I had, up to that point, ridden eight straight hours in a single day, covering 140 miles. Once. Only once.

So I continued searching. Browsing through Netflix for cycling documentaries, Tour Divide caught my eyes. It's a grueling 2,745-mile mountain bike race that traverses the length of the Rocky Mountains from Canada to the Mexican border. Racers have to brave harsh weather, snowy conditions, and remote terrain. They looked miserable. Still, I reached out to the filmmaker and director, Mike Dion, over Twitter, telling him how inspired I was watching Tour Divide, and asking if I could get involved in his upcoming project.

Mike told me about a new bicycle race called the Trans America Bike Race. It runs along the 4,400-mile Trans America Bike Trail which starts in Oregon, weaves through the Cascade Mountains, the Rocky Mountains, the Great Plains, and the Appalachia, ending in Yorktown, a little colonial town in Virginia. Mike's friend and fellow bicycle enthusiast, Nathan Jones, was the brainchild behind the Trans America Bike Race. For more than 30 years, thousands of people have been riding the Trans America Bike Trail, but nobody had thought to organize a race around it. Finally, in December 2013, Nathan put the challenge on the web to see if anyone would be crazy enough to join him in the first ever Trans America Bike Race.

A self-supported race (no support vehicle, food and drinks handed to you; each rider carries his or her own gear throughout the entire ride), there is no registration fee (the Race Across America costs $2,500). There are no checkpoints or support stations, just a start and end point and a designated route; everything in between is entirely up to the wits and discretion of the cyclist. And that was how I discovered a cycling world driven purely by the love of the sport.

Word of the inaugural Trans America Bike Race spread, and more than a hundred cyclists had signed up by the time I caught wind of it through Mike.

||||||||||||||||||

I clicked "Submit". I was the 129th crazy registrant. I beamed with pride.

Then I got worried. I had not consulted my husband beforehand, had not mentioned a bicycle race, much less one that was 4,400 miles long.

I'm often brash like that, exasperating my husband because then he has to rein me in when I commit to things that I have not given much thought to.

In some ways, I am grateful that I was impulsive and signed up for the Trans America Bike Race without first consulting my mind or my husband because if I had given it any more thought, I might never have cycled across America at all. Even as I think about it now, I realize how huge the goal was!

About the Trans America Bike Trail

The Trans America Bike Trail was developed from the blueprint of the Bikecentennial '76, a bicycle tour across the United States in the summer of 1976, in commemoration of the bicentennial of America's Declaration of Independence. The trail runs between Astoria, Oregon, and Yorktown, Virginia, and passes through many landmark and historic sites while avoiding major highways, high-traffic zones and big cities.

day 11 Encounter: Joanna Abernathy

I noticed a bicycle propped against the wall outside the only cafe open that early in the morning. Wisdom, Montana is so small it has only two motels and two restaurants, one of which we were headed into for breakfast.

I thought it was Eric's bike. Eric was a cross-country cyclist Derek and I had been seeing on and off along the same route. Unlike us, Eric carried all his essentials to camp and survive in the wilderness for several weeks. He was a mobile home on two wheels. He had his sleeping bag, pad, tent, cooking stove, cans of soup and beans, bottles of condiments, fresh fruits, and several liters of water. I have no idea how he cycled with all that weight. His fully loaded pannier bags clung securely but bulged on both rear sides of his bicycle.

Eric's bike would have taken up most of the space in the little town of Wisdom. We walked in, hoping to find Eric devouring two big plates of stacked-high pancakes. Instead, we found a stout woman in her 40s sitting in the far corner of the cafe, and a man in his late 50s sitting at a table next to her. They were chatting like old friends.

We took a seat at the table closest to them. A little town gossip wouldn't hurt. Besides, we were wondering what had happened to Eric and thought maybe they would know.

After we had placed our orders of the usual – two pancakes, a sunny-side up egg, and a cup of coffee for me; omelette, toast, and a cup of orange juice for Derek – there was still no sight of Eric. Could the bicycle belong to either the man or woman?

The man was wearing a cotton buttoned-up shirt and jeans. The woman was dressed in a loose black top and black pants. Then I spotted a bicycle helmet resting on the table next to her plate of food.

We asked if the bicycle outside belonged to her. She chirpily responded yes with an Aussie accent and broke into the warmest and most radiant smile.

She was bright and glowing. I couldn't tell if it was the film of oil on her skin or the sun's rays streaming into the cafe through the window near where she sat.

While we had a horribly cold and wretched time riding over the steep and snowy peaks of Chief Joseph Pass, arriving in Wisdom past 9:00 p.m., Joanna Abernathy, we later learned, didn't arrive in Wisdom until 1:00 a.m. She had hauled a loaded 50-pound bike up Chief Joseph Pass with slow and dogged determination.

"Wasn't that just utterly miserable?" I gulped, referring to the laborious climb, freezing cold, heavy load, and late arrival in town. Any two of those variables would have broken many cyclists, much less all four.

"Nah, I just went slow and focused on every single pedal. I had to keep pedaling or I'd slide backwards! My bags were so heavy! Cars were honking at me but I didn't care. I was just happy to be cycling."

"I'm riding in honor of Dr Martin Luther King," she went on. "I was a little girl of 14 when I saw his stirring 'I have a dream' speech in Washington D.C. He gave hope to millions of people. I was truly inspired. I'm riding now, as an adult, in tribute to him. I started in Astoria, Oregon and hope to finish on the steps of the Washington Capitol building."

Joanna handed us her calling card. On it was a quote by Dr King and her blog site.

I didn't ask any more questions. I didn't have to. She'd proven to me how much she was enjoying her ride with a positive outlook while I'd been beating myself down with a sour attitude.

Our breakfast arrived and we ate quickly as we had another long day ahead of us. In between huge bites of pancakes and eggs, we overheard the man telling Joanna that she should tell others about her adventure through social media. He was teaching her the nuts and bolts of setting up a Facebook page. Occasionally I'd glance back at Joanna and could see her smiling sweetly back at him, though I had the feeling his intentions were misguided. Like us, Joanna just wanted to get on her bike and ride. He was holding her back. Still, Joanna never betrayed her impatience.

I remembered that warm and enduring face as we got up to leave.

Three months later, I found out on Facebook that Joanna was knocked dead on the road in Indiana, just five days away from her destination in Washington where she would have concluded her epic ride in tribute to Dr King.

day 11 **Dillon**

In a state like Montana, where there is more wildlife than there are human beings per square mile, I was astonished to find casinos on every street corner. They were not the grand and glamorous types you find in Las Vegas; rather, they were integrated into every type of establishment – truck stops, restaurants, cafes, and convenience stores –

a couple of machines with flashing light bulbs in a dingy corner of a narrow hallway.

In Dillon, what seemed like a convenience store in a gas station also operated as a cafe, serving fresh-off-the-grill, hot breakfasts of burgers, omelettes and burritos, and when I ventured further back into the store to use the restroom, I found some 20 poker machines occupied by a handful of bored old men.

A quick research on my phone revealed that Montana has more than 1,400 licensed gambling operators and over 16,000 video gambling (a.k.a. jackpot) machines.

I was curious. Why were there so many casinos in Montana?

I would later find out that given its harsh and remote wilderness, Montana isn't ideal for agriculture or manufacturing as many other Midwestern states are. Casinos were a quick and effective way of increasing tax revenue and creating jobs.

Riding through Montana, I observed nothing close to a thriving economy. The men and women who gathered at these casinos and poker machines didn't look at all wealthy or happy – they carried with them a certain dullness and dejection, in stark contrast to the beauty of the Bitterroot Mountain range, snowcapped even in the summertime, with fly fishermen honing their skills along its rivers.

Riding through Nevada City, Montana, a former gold mining town.

Responsibility to Film

The Oregon Coast. The Rocky Mountains. Yellowstone. The plains of Kansas. The Appalachian Mountains of West Virginia. Not only would I be seeing these amazing natural landscapes, I would be passing through classic American towns, taking in the local flavor, chatter, and gossip at gas stations, convenience stores, and cafes.

I knew that as a sojourning cyclist pedaling at 15 mph, I would be getting the most out of my time and experience.

Perhaps more important than the sights, I really wanted to capture human stories. I love real life stories. I love to interact with and listen to others share their stories, struggles, triumphs, joys and tears, to know what lifted them and what broke them. I was convinced that if I were to cycle across America and travel through some 200 towns, surely I would be meeting many different people, and there might be several who would talk to me and share their stories.

I wanted to document everything I saw, experienced, and encountered, and share that with the world. I didn't want to cycle across America, and forget about it when I was done and dusted.

Cycling across America and experiencing her beauty was a great privilege, one which I didn't take lightly, and one which I knew I had to share.

Search for Film Crew

I started binging on sports documentaries on Netflix and YouTube. I made notes on what I liked and didn't like about each documentary. I picked and chose the elements I wanted in mine.

I also started scouting for a camera crew. After a few initial inquiries into the prices of local videographers, I was taken aback at how costly they were.

Searching for alternatives, I came across elance.com, an online marketplace where freelancers list their services and get discovered for short-term projects (Elance.com has since been acquired and is now Upwork.com). I immediately signed up to join the community and crafted my pitch, injecting zeal into it and hoping to attract potential videographers who would share my enthusiasm.

Here's what I wrote, word for word:

I'll be cycling across the country from June 7 to July 17.

During these 40 days, I need a driver and a videographer to follow me as I cycle from Astoria, Oregon to Yorktown, Virginia. I'll pay you $5,000 to travel across the country with me, and pay for all your meals and lodging. That would work out to be $9,000 in pay, meals and lodging (you bring home $5,000).

I'll hire a driver separately (if you know someone who might fit the bill, let me know).

We'll travel 100 miles each day and stay the night in a motel (separate rooms, of course).

I am crowdfunding this project on Kickstarter, and it'll be a pretty cool adventure to document the bike ride, stunning shots of the great American landscape, as well as people I will encounter and interview along the way.

If you have experience with filming documentaries and are good with composition, lighting and have tons of creativity, as well as a great personality, you'll fit the job really well.

I'll be happy for us to do a few Google Hangout sessions to assess our comfort level of going on this crazy 40-day adventure together.

Warning: I'll be riding 12-14 mph (I usually ride faster, but because I have to ride over 100 miles each day over 40 days, I need to ride much slower in order to sustain the entire trip) – which means, you may feel terribly bored sometimes at the slow speed when you're filming from the car, driving at 12-14 mph.

Think about it and write me if you are interested!

||||||||||||||

It was close to 11:30 p.m. and I was getting ready for bed.

Ten minutes later I got a response. I was ecstatic. I read the first line and my heart sank. It went:

I don't mean to burst your bubble but I'm sure you'll appreciate my honesty. I think you're insane. No one will shoot for you for $9,000. You'll have to double, triple that amount before you'll find yourself a decent videographer.

That message worried me. Would I not be able to find videographers willing to come on a project that might not be rewarding financially but sure would be rewarding experientially? Is this world we're living in really all about money and nothing more?

I went to bed dejected.

The next morning, I awoke and checked my phone. 25 new messages in my Elance inbox!

I scanned through the heading of each message and they were all positive – 25 interested videographers! A far cry from the critic the previous night.

Sam and Tom

Sam wore a black cap on his head of spiky blonde hair, looking every bit the creative artist that he was. Tom had smooth blond hair which fell somewhat messily on the sides and front of his head, and which he swiped up with his hand rather frequently.

We "met" for the first time on a Google conference call.

It was 10:00 p.m. in San Francisco where I was, and 6:00 a.m. in Milan where they were. I was trying my best to look decent and presentable, despite dressed in my pajamas. I could tell that it was the earliest call they had taken with a client. Sam, an early bird, had just finished a short run, while Tom pinched himself awake. A good start, I thought to myself, because I love early risers, being one myself.

From that first video call to subsequent calls and countless emails, Sam and Tom were enthusiastic and committed. They responded to my barrage of questions and suggestions with grace, patiently working with me as we plotted the story flow and shoot scenes. I could be in over my head sometimes, my thoughts and ideas racing at 100mph while what I really needed was someone to rein me in when I was in danger of going off track.

What impressed me about them was their eye for details.

It was obvious, from their point-by-point responses to my emails, that they read every word I wrote.

Sam is a punk rock bassist who started singing and writing songs since he was a kid in high school. Raised in Australia, Sam discovered his passion in music early on and immersed himself headlong into it. He self-produced his first music album with his brother Matt on drums, and a good friend on the guitar. Sam and his band, The Dirt Radicals, toured Southeast Asia frequently, performing in Singapore, Tokyo and Jakarta.

Tom, a graphic designer, grew up in Oxford, England.

"Everybody in Oxford attended Oxford University," he informed me. "Oh, is that right?" I was impressed.

A minute later I found out that he was kidding. Ah, the English sense of humor. Over the course of the next few months, we went over the storyline of the documentary, the scenes to shoot, potential characters, and nailed down the logistics.

Financial Hurdle

It could have been a cheaper affair, if I had merely ridden my bicycle and not filmed a documentary.

Or, even if I had wanted to capture the journey on film, I could have bike-packed to keep the cost low. Rather than sleeping in motels ($60-$90 a night), I could have carried my sleeping gear and slept in a tent on mostly free or cheap campgrounds. I could have filmed everything myself with a compact camera or several GoPro cameras attached to different parts of my bicycle.

But I wanted to produce a professional film to document a journey I could share with and use to inspire others.

And I wanted to make sure that I would last the distance and weeks by traveling light (without camping gear) and having adequate rest each night.

Without camping gear, I would need to stay in motels.

Besides, after the physical demand and exertion of cycling a full day, the reward of a hot shower and proper rest in a bed each night would recharge and refresh me for the subsequent days' ride.

Now, staying in a motel every night for 40 nights would cost a lot of money. On top of that, I would have to pay for the camera crew's accommodation.

It is cheap to dream but expensive to act on a dream. I knew my biggest hurdle would be financial. But I wasn't going to let money come between me and my dream.

Wyoming

day 14 **Yellowstone**

4:00 a.m. We rolled our bicycles out of the motel into the dark street. It was bitterly cold.

Derek and I had agreed on this early start to make up for the short mileage the day before where we had battled a strong headwind and covered a mere 77 miles. Besides, we wanted ample time today to see Yellowstone — the first national park in the world and one of the largest with the most diverse wildlife and ecosystem in the United States.

My front light worked for several yards and then suddenly went out. Derek didn't have any front light at all. Thankfully we were still in town, and not several miles in the deep woods of Yellowstone where there would be no shops or amenities for a long way.

We stumbled across the street to a gas station to buy replacement batteries for my worn ones.

As luck would have it, the gas station was closed. It opens for business at 6:00 a.m. We should have known.

We couldn't ride in the dark. Not when we were headed into the woods.

We had no choice but to try to get the light to work. Perhaps it wasn't that the batteries were out of juice? Perhaps I didn't align the batteries in the right + and - order?

A former bicycle mechanic and obviously the more handy of us both, Derek unscrewed the cap, took the batteries out, blew into the light, as if to clean off any dust, made sure he aligned the batteries in the right order, screwed the cap, and pressed the "On" button.

And there was light! We slapped high-fives, I praised Derek's brilliance to the sky, he blushed red even in the dark, and we quickly got on our way, in case the light chose to go out again.

Between us we had only an apple and a stick of honey. There was a lodge in the national park just 30 miles ahead. The plan was to ride to the lodge for breakfast and carry on cycling and exploring the park. What we didn't know was how cold the ride would be and how a lack of food plus low temperatures would drastically slow down our average pace, so even 30 miles felt like a long, long way.

Barely 10 miles into our ride I was weak with hunger. Several times I was tempted to stop passing RVs (recreational vehicles) to ask if they would offer us some of their leftover food. Surely a driver would have food - bread, sandwiches, a piece of fruit, perhaps. But I sensed Derek would be embarrassed and held my tongue.

Finally, 16 long miles later, we got to a campground and stopped to use the restroom. Driven by desperation, I approached a pair of women near the restroom.

We were cyclists riding across the country, I explained, and we were hungry. Would they have anything at all they could offer to tide us through to the next available cafe or restaurant?

"Why yes, certainly! You poor things must be starving!" one of them exclaimed. While one made us peanut butter jelly sandwiches, the other offered us biscuits and chips, which I devoured like a ravenous beast in the wild. There's no shame in hunger, I told myself. I was operating in survival mode.

Recharged, we thanked the ladies profusely and bid them farewell before hopping back on our bicycles.

As we rode, we noticed hot geysers spouting up on our left and right – we had ridden right into the famous geyser basin in Yellowstone! (I later found out that Yellowstone is home to 60% of the world's geysers).

We stopped one too many times to snap shots of the geysers, before arriving at the Old Faithful Lodge where we made a stop for a second round of breakfast: pancakes, burritos, country potatoes, coffee, and orange juice.

We were still feeling cold from our morning encounter so we stayed longer than we should have, soaking in the comfort and warmth of the posh restaurant as we enjoyed our breakfast. I wished we didn't have some 70 miles ahead of us. I think silently we each wished we could have stayed there for most of the day.

Yet the mission ahead beckoned so we got up to leave. As we stepped out into the sunshine, we noticed a crowd gathered at the far end of a platform. Curious, we rode

Old Faithful, one of the most famous geysers in America.

▲ Morning Glory Pool geyser.

our bikes closer. Scores of people were waiting. Some were sitting on the benches shaped like horseshoes, while some stood around, chatting or taking photographs. Derek asked a gentleman what people were waiting for.

"Old Faithful!" he exclaimed. "The famous geyser of Yellowstone! He's showing up soon. You should stay and watch." He winked.

Derek and I looked at each other. We had indeed allowed time today to "sight-see" Yellowstone. This would be too epic an event to miss, especially since we were right there at Old Faithful!

Named in 1870 by Henry D. Washburn, a U.S. representative from Indiana and a general in the Union Army during the Civil War, Old Faithful is one of the most predictable geographical features on earth, erupting every

▲ Red Spouter geyser.

60 to 110 minutes, to heights up to 180 feet.

And then it happened. A gush of hot bubbling geyser spouted from the ground into the sky, to the gasps and cheers of an appreciative crowd. Derek and I whipped out our phone cameras to record the phenomenon. I was in awe. For a brief moment, I almost forgot the misery of the past days.

Throughout the day, we made frequent stops to revel in Yellowstone's glory.

By late afternoon, we had crossed from Yellowstone to the Grand Teton National Park. Jackson Lake laid between us and the majestic Grand Teton (13,775 feet, second highest peak in the state of Wyoming, after Gannett Peak, 13,809 feet), outlined against the canvas of the blue sky by her rugged snowcapped peaks.

View of Jackson Lake with the Teton mountain range in the background.

day 15 Encounter: Adam

Following the spectacular wonder of Yellowstone, life for Derek and I rolled back into motion. It was business as usual – waking up early and pedaling until our legs hurt.

We set off at 5:00 a.m., and rode tirelessly from Moran to Dubois, covering 56 miles and over 3,000 feet in elevation.

We did that on empty stomachs from morning until late afternoon; there were no places to stop for food between. Our energy tanks were severely depleted and our pace suffered. We took almost twice as much time as usual to cycle just 56 miles.

Our spirits dipped until we got to a gas station where we met a gregarious bunch of cross-country cyclists. Adam, a ginger-haired guy with a Fu Manchu mustache, bright orange jersey, and yellow polka dotted neck band, stood out because of his smile.

I had never seen a smile more sincere, boyish, and happy. He kept saying, "Man, this is awesome," and grinned non-stop. I was hoping he wouldn't require a response from me but he turned to me and asked, "Isn't this just awesome?"

I didn't want to disappoint, and failing to match his enthusiasm, simply forced out a weak nod and said, "Yeah." I was lying of course, but in his excitement, he didn't notice.

We ordered pizza from the gas station, which to our amazement was baked fresh in the store. While we waited for our slices, I watched Adam with his bright smile and positive countenance. I thought to myself, how can this guy be so happy? How can anyone be so happy? How can the bike ride be so awesome? What is he doing that I'm not doing? How was I experiencing so much misery while he experienced so much joy?

The difference was Adam and company were riding 60 miles a day while Derek and I rode 100. They had the luxury of taking their time and enjoying the ride, something that I didn't have the time or money to do. I was envious, but I had built a box of self-imposed restrictions, stepped right into it, and got mad that nobody came to rescue me.

day 15 **Who Would Have Thought?**

It's the little things that either make or break you.

In all of my research before taking off on the ride, I had no idea that in the summer months in the Rocky Mountains, your number one enemy may, yes, be the snow, but there is an enemy even greater than the snow.

Mosquitoes.

How was I to know to look out for mosquitoes? You don't know what you don't know. I don't know who coined that term but he or she must have had a lot of surprises in his or her life.

I was rudely awakened by the fact that there could be that many mosquitoes in one small area.

Mosquitoes breed in Wyoming and Colorado from June to July.

Perfect timing. My ride was between June and July.

I literally rode into the epicenter of mosquito breeding season, at the height of summer.

Sure, steep hill climbs, loneliness on the road and bad weather had taken its toll on me, but mosquitoes? That was the straw that broke the camel's back.

For five straight days, Derek and I rode with an entourage of vicious mosquitoes. We were given the royal treatment – they made us feel like VIPs as they surrounded and escorted us every pedal of the way. It was impossible to stop to take a break – we had to keep pedaling, and to pedal fast, or they'd attack every square inch of skin, exposed or clothed. Persistent and annoying, they were impossible to fend off. While they did make us go faster with fewer breaks, we were pushed to exhaustion day after day.

Debut Into Film

Emboldened by my dad, I was always asking "why this" and "why that". He was sure I would go somewhere with my curiosity. And by somewhere, he literally saw it as a place. In his mind, I would leave my homeland as an adult and make a name for myself in a foreign land.

I often look back and think about my dad's intentions when he named me Angeline, which means "bearer of truth" and Ai Fong, which means "to love the wind". Fast forward more than three decades, the wind literally took me under its wings, bringing me first from Malaysia to Singapore, and eventually landing me in America.

Despite being new to America and its cultural norms, I quickly observed that this country embraces the very thing my dad encouraged: asking questions. I began asking questions, and the more I asked, the bolder I became.

||||||||||||||||

What do you do when you don't know what to do? Ask.

I knew little about filmmaking, so I decided to reach out to the professionals in the field and ask if they might be interested in collaborating. The pros, I reckoned, would include broadcasters so I started making a list of the big names: National Geographic, BBC, Discovery, HBO, Lonely Planet and PBS.

Naively I thought I could easily scour through their websites for the criteria on film submission and make my pitch. Was I in for a rude surprise! The task at hand was so monumental it felt like searching for a needle in a haystack.

National Geographic does not accept unsolicited show proposals. The only way to get their attention is through an established production company.

BBC, Discovery, and HBO – there was no option of reaching the channels via their websites – I would have to find an inroad through one of their staff.

Lonely Planet had me fill out a web contact form which I hoped someone would read and channel to the right department.

PBS, I found out, doesn't produce programs, which meant I would have to produce the documentary myself, and only then would PBS consider my film.

So I made a second list: television production houses I could partner with. Making lists and scanning websites for preliminary information is easy; finding the right person in charge and getting their contact details is the hard part.

I found press releases on their sites, which usually included contact information for the head of public relations or communications. What I was really interested in was the email format. Say the email address reads: angelinetan@google.com. In this case, the email format of the company would most likely be firstnamelastname@companyname.com. With that, I was able to guess the email address of the person I wanted to reach.

Of course, that wasn't always the case. Sometimes the email format varies between individuals in the same company. I almost never got it right, despite trying some 20 email variations. Each outbound email attempt would return to me with an "invalid email address" notice.

I also signed up for LinkedIn's premium membership so I could send messages to people outside my network. For a month, I sent as many messages as I could to decision makers in companies I wanted to collaborate with. At the end of a month, I discontinued my membership and moved on to Twitter.

On Twitter, I read people's updates and tried to leave a clever comment or two, in the hopes that they might take note of me, and carry on the conversation. After a few conversation exchanges, I'd bring up the subject of collaboration. If they saw a potential partnership, they would ask me to email them with more details. That always made my day.

I worked hard to draft effective emails, carefully selecting each word and sentence. Many high level executives have their email inbox flooded with requests and messages from people they don't know. I had to grab their attention with a punchy subject line and interesting message.

Meticulously, I kept a detailed list of the companies I wrote to and followed up with them.

This process was time consuming and emotionally draining. I put my heart and soul into each outreach effort, anticipated a response, and waited.

Nothing.

I waited some more. Silence.

After a few months of doing this, I was in the slumps, ready to throw in the towel. But a small voice within tugged at me, "If no broadcasters or production houses would produce the documentary, why don't you do it yourself?"

That's not a bad idea, I thought. Yes, why don't I?

Corporate Sponsorship

I have a simplistic view of funding. It should be available and accessible as long as the objectives of both the funder (a sponsor company) and fund seeker (in this case, me) are aligned.

Many companies today have budgets for event sponsorships. They do this to increase their visibility in the public eye, build goodwill among current and prospective customers and ultimately, boost revenue.

I believed that my ride, with its aim of inspiring others into action and pursuing their dreams would advance a potential sponsor's goals.

Armed with this confidence, I reached out to various big

companies including GoPro, Google, Yahoo, various banks, and cycling apparel and sports nutrition manufacturers. I tracked the founders and heads of marketing and public relations on Twitter and LinkedIn and sent them private messages.

Day after day, I'd craft personalized emails to various companies, pitching them about the benefits of sponsoring my ride.

Despite what I thought was a smart email strategy, I didn't hear back from the companies I wrote to. Perhaps I didn't do it right. Perhaps I was trying too hard to sell myself with little consideration for the companies' objectives and what was in it for them.

I kept writing. It was often discouraging, but I kept at it. I reckoned the more emails I sent out, the higher my chances of getting a response.

After several months I secured several product sponsorships:

Total Cycle Coach (UK) where Coach Colin Batchelor single-handedly transformed me from an amateur into an ultra distance cyclist.

Apidura (UK) sponsored the bags and packs I had on my bike – I love them because the bags could easily be attached to any bike without a metal bicycle rack like traditional pannier bags require. The founder of Apidura, Tori Fahey, is herself an ultra endurance cyclist and backpacker and understands the need for lightweight and easily-attachable bags for long distance rides.

Voler Apparel (US) provided me with three complete

sets of cycling apparel of my choice. When a faulty zipper fell off my lightweight rain jacket in Idaho, I contacted Voler and they immediately mailed me a new jacket so I could keep warm in the rain and snow in the Pacific Northwest.

Osmo Hydration (US) provided me with huge quantities of liquid nutrition and hydration.

I was elated that these companies took a chance on me, an unknown athlete and newbie to the world of ultra endurance cycling.

While the product sponsorships helped to offset some of the cost, I still needed money for airfare, accommodations, and food. I wrote to the first hotel I'd be staying at in Astoria. I didn't manage to secure a free night's stay.

I was getting desperate. The doors weren't opening as I had hoped they would. With my back pressed to the wall, I realized that I would have to pry open a door for myself. That was when I decided to raise funds the grassroots way, via Kickstarter.

Crowd Funding

Imagine a world where everybody supported everyone in their endeavors, big or small. Build an electric bicycle, produce a music album, write a book, design and manufacture a multi-pocketed traveling vest.

Money is essential to living and realizing dreams. And funding can be found, if you know where to look. Kickstarter is where the courageous initiator or creator of a project positions his pitch to evoke a response from potential contributors: "Here's a little bit of money. Go make that happen."

For my Kickstarter campaign, I needed a short but witty pitch, a good video, and rewards which ranged from simple thank you emails and virtual high-fives to digital downloads of the full film and mentions of corporate sponsors in the closing credits of the film.

I studied successful campaigns for projects similar to mine and wrote to friends and strangers who have successfully launched and funded Kickstarter projects.

I used Twitter and LinkedIn extensively to reach out to people who had gone before me and succeeded.

During this process, I realized that people are more willing to share than we think they are. They have received help themselves, so they are more than happy to help others.

I finally launched my campaign on a Thursday in April 2014. Thursday is the best day to launch a new campaign because people are typically overwhelmed by the demands of work on Monday and Tuesday after the weekend; come Wednesday, things start to slow a little; and by Thursday, people are more relaxed and open to new content on the web and in their inboxes.

The first few contributions came from friends.

I learned firsthand that if you want to do anything, you must persist and plow through.

Persist – I made a long list of potentially supportive friends and kept adding to it. I wrote catchy email subject headings, made the opening paragraph of the email about the receiver's interest rather than mine, and kept my pitch short and to the point. People are more likely to respond to personal messages than generic ones. I'd send 50 personal messages a day via email and Facebook messenger. I sent reminders, twice, three times, and stopped. There is a thin line between persistence and what I will call "pest-sistance".

Plow through – if one friend didn't contribute, I tried another. I asked them to share the link and looked for other ways to share the project. I wrote to bloggers and influential personalities and asked them to spread news about my project.

No success is left to chance. If I wanted it, I had to plan and work for it. Successful Kickstarter projects are usually a result of careful planning, strategy, and execution. Execution is more important than just strategy.

Even though I did all I could, and in hindsight I could have tried even harder and written more emails, word about my project was not spreading fast enough.

30 days in and my Kickstarter campaign did not manage to raise my goal of $40,000. I had only managed to raise $12,000.

‖‖‖‖‖‖‖‖‖‖‖‖‖

When my Kickstarter campaign failed to raise the funds I needed, I started to look for alternatives.

I had become disenchanted with both Kickstarter and its popular competitor, Indiegogo.

Kickstarter has an all-or-nothing funding policy – either you raise the full amount you need within a certain timeframe (upon which Kickstarter charges a 5% fee) or you don't get a single dollar pledged by your "backers". Say my goal was to raise $40,000. If I successfully raised the full sum, Kickstarter charges $2,000 for its service.

Indiegogo, on the other hand, has a flexible funding policy where you get to keep every dollar pledged by your backers. At that point in time, Indiegogo charged 9% when you don't reach your goal (it has since reduced the fee to 5%).

Both platforms are costly and have their own limitations.

Then, out of the blue, a co-founder from a new competitor to the crowdfunding space, Ignition Deck, reached out to me.

Ignition Deck costs only $79 to get started, I get to keep every pledged dollar, plus I get to determine how long I want to run each campaign for (Kickstarter and Indiegogo usually cap each campaign to 30 days).

In order to shift my Kickstarter backers to Ignition Deck, I reached out to each of my backers via a personal email message, explaining the shortfall in Kickstarter and how the amount they pledged wasn't at all credited from their bank account and will they please make a fresh contribution on my website via the Ignition Deck plugin I've installed.

During this time, I learned an interesting thing. The people you thought would support you didn't, and the people you didn't expect to, did. A banker-triathlete in Singapore who heard of my campaign via a mutual friend, pledged $500 at first, then raised it to $2,000. Such generosity from a total stranger. He eventually became a good friend and advisor, and still is today.

My in-laws, though they didn't understand why I had to cycle across America, why I had to spend all this money to "inspire someone else," and though they were constantly worried for my safety, contributed several thousand dollars.

My frugal mom pledged $300. You must understand, she

lives in Malaysia, where $300 (at that time) in the U.S. was like $1,000 in Malaysia.

And while I had tried so hard for several months to raise cash sponsorships from companies to no avail, a few weeks before the start of the ride, two Singaporean companies donated a generous sum of money to my ride. Muvee is a movie-editing software company and Infinitum Robotics specializes in unmanned aerial systems company (drone applications).

And this was how, with just a week left before the start of the ride, I raised $23,000. I was thrilled! It was a large sum of money, and I was grateful to every individual and company who believed and "invested" in me.

At this point I was still $17,000 short. I hadn't managed to raise all $40,000 needed to finance the ride and film the documentary. Undeterred, I left for Astoria. You can't always wait for the right time to do something. Sometimes you must make a leap of faith.

Ghost Towns

The United States is so vast that riding from one town to another can feel like you're entering a different planet altogether. Some towns are bustling with people and activities; some are eerily quiet with shops shut tight and deserted streets. Some are plainly abandoned.

Sometimes I saw the brick and wooden frames of houses lying exposed to the elements. Sometimes trucks, tractors, grain mills, and plowing equipment were left right where they were – intact but claimed by weeds and rust.

These scenes looked uncannily like something out of apocalyptic films where foreign spaceships descended on earth to wipe out all of humanity, leaving worldly materials as they were. Maybe Hollywood producers get some of their inspiration from these abandoned towns.

There were bound to be a few ghost towns in every state we rode through. I can only describe the feeling of approaching and riding through those towns in two words: utter despondence. A heavy air of sadness would swallow us whole as we rode. Neither of us would speak. We would each be absorbed in our own thoughts, wondering silently what happened in the town's heyday.

We didn't feel the need to stop or explore either – there was nothing for us there. The past holds no appeal to a pair of passing cyclists. We simply rode on, eagerly anticipating the sight of the next living person.

day 17 Jeffrey City: Party of One

The most distinctive ghost towns in my memory were not fully "dead" but had a semblance of life, or intentional restorative efforts.

After cycling six straight hours, Derek and I were desperate for a place to stop for lunch. We had set off from Lander, Wyoming at 6:00 a.m. We typically stopped for a small bite every two to three hours, but there was nothing in between the long stretch from Lander to Sweetwater Station, a former watering hole for horses.

We rode for another two hours in anticipation of Jeffrey City. We were hopeful that a place with "city" in its name might signify a large population and plenty of places to find food.

Approaching an almost obscured sign for Jeffrey City, our hearts sank. The area was dry and barren. There was a handful of abandoned buildings. There wasn't anyone on the street. This was no city!

We came to a stop in front of what looked like a permanently closed liquor shop. The beer posters plastered on its windows were peeling and tattered. Derek got off his bike and walked to the door.

"It's open!" Derek exclaimed.

I was skeptical. I walked closer and peeped in. It sure was open, and it wasn't a liquor store, but a restaurant with tables and chairs!

I could have sworn I did a little jig as I walked through its cowboy-tavern-like doors.

A man emerged from behind the bar counter wearing a dark blue apron over his dirty grey T-shirt and blue jeans.

"Oh, hello there, how can I help you?" he asked, with a thick drawl. His eyes were barely opened and he sported a multiple-day unshaved mustache.

"Can we order some food?" Derek asked expectantly.

"Sure." He handed us a one-page paper menu. The selection was pretty standard – burgers or sandwiches with fries, a salad or two, and some side items.

As we studied the simple menu, the man went on, "Man, I'm so hungover. We had a great party last night. Lots of drinking. Lots of dancing. Partied til 1:00 a.m. Geez, that was pretty wild."

Derek and I looked at each other. We looked around the restaurant. There was nobody there except for us three. Outside, the town looked like it had just survived a nuclear attack. There wasn't another soul inside or outside the restaurant. What party was he talking about?

We assumed him drunk, and fixed our eyes on the menu.

"Oh, don't bother looking at the menu. We only serve chicken burgers at this moment."

"Erm, okay, we'll have a chicken burger each. It comes with fries, right?" Derek decided for us both.

"Yeah, regular fries or sweet potato fries?" the man asked.

Derek was about to answer when the man interrupted him, "Oh sorry, fella, we only have regular fries. That alright with you?"

"Yes," Derek smiled.

The man disappeared behind the counter to the kitchen.

Derek and I looked at each other and laughed. Quietly, of course, in case he emerged from the kitchen. We didn't want to offend the man preparing our lunch.

We agreed that the man must be Jeffrey, because he was the only man in town. We also agreed that he was a little mad, because he must have imagined the party in his head.

We ate our lunch hungrily, paid up, and left.

||||||||||||||

In hindsight, I understand why I reacted that way to ghost towns. I lived for over 16 years in the vibrant and stellar island-state of Singapore. Singapore constantly undergoes development at such a dizzying pace that its skyline changes form and shape every year. Even its geography changes, as it furiously claims more of the ocean and piles sand onto its boundaries to artificially build more "land". If you lived in Singapore for a year, left for five years and returned to visit, you would find it hard to recognize any part of it at all.

I was projecting the rapid growth of Singapore onto America, which is 13,800 times larger (Singapore measures a mere 277 square miles in land size, while the U.S. spans an enormous 3.8 million square miles).

I was used to progression, not regression. Although I had expected to encounter small towns during my ride, I hadn't expected to run into so many ghost towns.

▲ Hoosier Pass, in the Rocky
Mountains of central Colorado.
Hoosier Pass marks the highest point
of my ride, at 11,500 feet.

Colorado

Only a Mile to Go!

As cyclists, we learn to take others' words with a pinch of salt. This is especially true when talking to fellow cyclists who are cruising downhill in the opposite direction while we're climbing uphill. The pain is intense during uphill climbs, but quickly forgotten at the peak, where labored breathing and grunts are traded for relieved sighs and victorious smiles. When we cruise downhill, we put the earlier pain of climbing uphill behind us, and we forget the effort, distance, and time it took us to get from the bottom of the hill to the top. So when we head downhill and someone climbing up in the opposite direction asks, in between gasps of air, how much farther to the top, in our euphoria (or oblivion), we holler, "not too far now, less than a mile or so, you're almost there!"

Initially, in my earlier years as a cyclist, I believed every word. "Not too far to go, less than a mile away, I've got this." I would pedal as quickly as I could, hoping to get there in my personal best time.

Many times, as we climbed steep passes in the Rocky Mountains and asked descending cyclists the distance to the peak, we would hear the usual "only a mile to go".

I have learned to add another mile or two to their responses, having been tricked, worn my legs out, and had my spirit crushed one too many times.

day 21 **Oh So Drained**

In the middle of a busy highway just a few miles outside of Pueblo, I rode over a small rock in the middle of the road shoulder. My tire punctured and lost air immediately. It must have been the strain from the heavy saddle pack on my thin 23mm tire. For racing or short distance cycling, 23mm tires would have been perfect. For ultra distances with extra weight, 23mm wouldn't do the job. A flat tire was inevitable. I spent 10 minutes fixing the flat, as cars zoomed past us.

Flat fixed, we continued pedaling. Our morale was low as the temperature started to rise. We made more stops than usual at gas stations along the way for cold coconut water.

Kansas was 172 miles ahead of us. Our goal for the day was to get as close to Kansas as possible.

And then the wind hit, sudden and strong. It felt like we had ridden into a wind tunnel and there was no other way around it. We had to forge ahead.

As hard as I tried, I wasn't making much progress. I was riding along Highway 96 next to a railroad track. A cargo train was making its way west, in the opposite direction. The train was incredibly long. Mile after mile of car after car of cargo passed me at what I perceived to be a slow pace. I tried to set a goal for myself – at least try to get to the next intersection before the train disappeared out of sight.

I must have ridden next to that never-ending train for ten minutes before it finally left me for good.

The wind kept at us. We kept trying to inch forward, but the wind pushed us back. Instead of averaging our usual 16 mph, we were laboring at a mere 10 mph. By attempting to cover the same distance at a slower pace, we had to add an extra four hours to our day.

Mentally, we were drained. To listen to the unceasing howl of the wind in your ears as you ride headlong into resistance, to labor longer than you normally would in better conditions – it was exhausting. And discouraging.

If there was any consolation at all, it was that the wind kept the scorching sun at bay. I felt a slight sense of gratitude to the wind for cooling off an otherwise incredibly hot day.

The sky got darker and darker until it was pitch black when we rolled into a tiny town in the middle of nowhere. Welcome to Ordway, read a rather prominent stone and steel sign by the intersection, dim in the evening light.

Derek and I had planned to cross into Kansas but the state line wasn't another 100 miles away. We had grossly overestimated our capacity to cover the distance and underestimated the resistance of Mother Nature.

Beaten, despondent and famished, with every shop and the only restaurant in town closed for the night, we found a grocery store about to shut its door, persuaded the cashiers to let us in, grabbed the most calorie-dense food we could find, Marie Callender's chicken pot pie, heated up our frozen pies for ten long minutes in the microwave and sat outside the store to devour our savory treat, washed down with a bottle of chocolate milk each.

Rest, Recharge, Reset

After each steep mountain pass where I'd climb to my breaking point and utter exhaustion, I realized that I hadn't grown any stronger; I'd simply tackled each mountain pass as it came. When faced with each climb, my first thought was, man that's diffcult, but when I approached it, I would find suffcient strength to handle it. Just when I thought I had given it my all and could not possibly ride the next day, I could.

I learned to rest, recharge, and reset. I might be depleted one day and wake up the next day feeling tired and crappy, but once I was on the road, a new leash of energy enabled me to keep going. Sure, pain might show up, horrible weather might come tumbling, and unforeseen situations might loom at unexpected intersections, but each new day would bring with it a fresh bag of resources to overcome the day's challenges. This may sound airy-fairy but the universe does conspire to lend you a helping hand when you're at your wits' end.[1]

day 22 **Managing Expectations**

Hoosier Pass stands lofty, its peak stretching 11,500 feet into the sky. I was halfway through the journey; there were 18 days to go.

[1] Adapted from Paulo Coelho's The Alchemist: "And when you want something, all the universe conspires in helping you to achieve it."

Up to that point, there wasn't a single day that went by without climbing.

As I stared at Hoosier Pass from the foothills, I remembered what I had been told by other cyclists who had ascended it – that the rest of the journey after that would be downhill until the plains of Kansas, Missouri, Illinois, Indiana, and Ohio, for a good several hundred miles until we got to the Appalachian mountains in Virginia.

Imagine my excitement as I pedaled up the pass – the misery would soon be over!

Derek and I summited Hoosier Pass, waved our hands in victory, posed for a photograph as proof of our endeavor, and proceeded to descend the mountain.

We rolled down a steep descent – screaming in excitement as we did, the painful days behind us already a memory.

I did the math in my mind: It took us three weeks to climb 11,500 feet. Kansas is only 1,500 feet above sea level. Surely the next 10,000 feet or so would just be a matter of gravity and momentum where we would have little pedaling to do, if at all.

How wrong I was!

The descent lasted but two hours, after which the terrain leveled out.

As we pedaled, I kept anticipating another descent. That descent never happened. We kept working our way forward.

I was puzzled, disappointed and angry. Whatever happened to "it's all downhill from here to Kansas"?

Later research would reveal that what goes up must indeed come down, but the degree to which it goes up doesn't necessarily equate to the degree it goes down. While the ascent to Hoosier Pass from the foothills of the Rocky Mountains in Idaho had been mostly steep with gradients between 6 and 10 degrees, the descent into Kansas was more gradual with gradients between 3 and 5 degrees.

Time Constraints

When I finally hit the road, I had only one concern: Was I physically able to ride 8 to 10 hours a day?

I was surprised when the challenges I faced had little to do with my physical ability, but were more about a battle against time, weather, and expectations.

Whenever you attempt something on a large scale, unforeseen circumstances will inevitably surface and throw you off course along the way. To coordinate a ride across a country, know that time will almost certainly be disrupted by the weather.

I had planned to ride eight hours, with two hours of breaks, so if we woke up at 5:00 a.m. and started riding at 6:00 a.m., we'd be done at 4:00 p.m. We could head into town, check out the diners, talk to some folks, and record some interviews.

It never happened according to plan.

The wind (headwinds especially), rain, snow, hail storms, and thunderstorms – these turned what should have been 10-hour days into 12- and sometimes 14-hour days. While ideally we should have completed the day by 4:00 p.m., we always ended between 6:00 and 8:00 p.m., which thankfully in the summer wasn't a problem because the days were long. It stayed bright until 9:15 p.m.

One reason for our long days was that we took long breaks in between. A little 10-minute stop here, a little 20-minute stop there, several times a day, and those usually added up to about four hours. If the weather was bad, we'd go slower, or be forced to take more breaks to seek shelter. Some days we wouldn't be done until 8:00 p.m.

My body would be tired from the ride as I saw cars zooming past, giving me a new appreciation for cars: They were invented to cut travel time. I knew this, of course, but this fact became more pronounced when I was traveling slower on a less time-efficient vehicle. What would take only an hour in a car would take up to six hours on a bicycle.

||||||||||||||||

One of my main goals for the ride was to meet people, chat with them, and hopefully, draw out an inspirational story or two from a war veteran perhaps, or a struggling migrant working multiple jobs to make ends meet. That was hard to do, because in order to chat with people and draw out deeply personal stories from them, it required time, and time was something I didn't have. I had to complete the ride each day before dark, and we made rest stops several times during the day. Derek loved to chat and I often had to drag him away from conversations he was having with the local folks because we had to hit the road.

I had only managed to raise enough money to cover expenses for 40 days and my camera crew had another assignment they had to leave for after 40 days. I wasn't able to stretch the trip longer.

I had initially wanted to ride across America to see the whole country, but the 13 states I cycled through did not comprise the entire United States. And I certainly didn't experience those 13 states fully.

Time pressure took the joy out of so many areas that could have made the ride more pleasant and memorable. We could have relished delectable food, ridden through fascinating places, talked to people, found out about the local culture, and enjoyed America more.

Lodging

Deciding to sleep in motels every night was the best decision I made, because it meant a few luxuries: a place to shower and wash my clothes, a warm bed to sleep in, and I wouldn't have to carry the extra weight of a sleeping bag, pad, and tent on my already loaded bicycle.

As good a decision as it was, it also came with a unique set of challenges. There wasn't always a town at each 100-mile marker.

Even if there was a town, there wouldn't always be a motel present or available. Some of the towns were so small, their populations were negligible. I came across populations of 10 and 20. These "towns" didn't have general stores, gas stations, or motels.

Some towns were a mere confluence of several houses, with a single road that ran between the houses. Often I wondered if anyone really lived in any of the houses. Not a single soul was to be seen around the houses or on the streets; not a sound could be heard.

Over the days and weeks, I realized that the best way to determine if a town had a motel was to see how big the town was. If the population was over 200, it would be a pretty safe bet that there would be a motel. At that point, I would have to cross my fingers and hope it wasn't fully booked!

day 22 **Encounter: Albert**

I walked into a gas station just outside of Ordway after a fitful night of rest.

An elderly man looked at me and decided he would speak to me. Of course I had no idea then that he was an angel in disguise, sent to rescue a weary soul.

"Where are you going?" he asked, curious. I got the impression there wasn't much cycling going on in this part of town.

"Virginia," I replied, a little unenthusiastically. I had a lot on my mind as I ordered breakfast – I was struggling to find motivation to keep riding and was concerned about running out of funds before we got to Virginia.

"You mean you're riding your bicycle to Virginia? Where did you start? Here?" He was really curious now.

"Oh no, we started in Oregon."

"My word! That's impressive, young lady! I can't even drive that far, let alone cycle."

I returned his compliment with a smile and was about to walk away when he went on, "See, I just had a heart bypass. Doctor told me I only have four months to live.

Cycling that far will only kill me faster," he chuckled to himself.

I stopped in my tracks and felt a pang in my heart. Here I was, worried about not completing the ride in 40 days, and here was a man, who had only four months to live.

We sat down to have breakfast together. He was a cattle rancher who owned several acres of farmland in Kansas where he worked his entire life before his health started failing. He had since passed the business on to his son. Even after his surgery with a few months left to live, he still goes to the ranch to work for several hours every morning. "You can take a horse out of the field but you can't take the work out of the horse," he told me.

The day we met was a Sunday.

"Are you going to work today?" I asked. "No, I'm going to church later."

"Can I pray for you, Albert?"

He was caught by surprise. "Yes, young lady, that would be lovely."

I closed my eyes, put my hand on his shoulder, and prayed for peace upon his heart to know that he was safe in God's hands, and for a miracle to heal him and prolong his life.

My encounter with Albert taught me a valuable lesson: Live everyday as if it were your last. And until the last day, do what you love. Albert enjoyed working on the ranch. His health might fail him, but he would continue to do what he loved until the day he could no longer do so.

Walking out of the gas station, I resolved to enjoy the

journey from there on, even if I did not have everything under control, particularly with funding.

Missing Home

By the second week, I was tired of being on the road. The drill was the same everyday: Wake up at 5:00 a.m., cycle for eight hours, check in to a motel in a local town at dusk, shower, wash my soiled clothes, hang them out to dry in the room, grab a quick dinner, drink Emergen-C (an effervescent drink – my favorite was the tangerine-flavored one), have an apple (to keep the doctor away – it worked!), stretch my legs, and sleep.

I disliked only riding my bicycle and not interacting with more people. When Derek and I rode on desolate roads, which was 70% of the time, it felt long and lonely. I enjoyed the views of the national forests, windy roads, rolling hills, snow-capped mountains, flowing rivers, streams, and creeks, but combined with derelict and frozen-in-time ghost towns, the feeling of isolation was rather acute.

I know cyclists who ride for the pleasure of solitude, but I realized I don't enjoy solitude in such huge doses.

Isn't it ironic then, that I chose to cycle across a continent where the journey is long, days are stretched, and copious periods of seclusion are expected?

I should have known better but I didn't prepare myself for it.

I was so homesick I envied the girl behind the counter in McDonald's or the local convenience store. At least she had a predictable routine of going to work, operating familiar tasks, and returning home to her family. She functioned in a familiar environment, while I didn't. Each day I would be unsure what the road or weather would throw at me, never certain if some unforeseen challenge might sneak up unannounced.

I ached for the certainty and comforts of home. I desperately wanted to quit the road and go home where I could see my husband everyday.

In a hazy stupor, I caught myself swimming in silly thoughts in my mind and snapped myself back to reality by thinking: "Here I am, having the adventure of my life, and I am envying the girl working in McDonald's." How crazy is that when that very girl could well be envying me, traveling across the United States, seeing beautiful sights and meeting new and different people and eating whatever I desired because I would burn the calories off on the ride.

Like they say, the grass isn't always greener on the other side. The grass is green where you are.

Doubts

Did I ever doubt I could cross the United States on my bicycle? I most certainly did, especially with the ambitious timeline that I had set for myself.

For a good six months before my ride in the summer of 2014, I was overcome with fear.

I remember an evening in February 2014 at the cinema with my husband. During the trailers before *Robocop*, my mood switched from joy to gloom. One of the upcoming movies, *Edge of Tomorrow*, starring Tom Cruise, was opening on June 6, 2014.

June 6, 2014.

Those words sprang up from the screen and sent a shudder down my spine. I suddenly found myself shaking on the inside. I became terribly afraid, because I knew that very week in June 2014, in fact a day after the release of that movie, I'd be leaving my daily comforts behind for a trip across the country.

I'd go to bed anxious each night. As I snuggled beneath the warmth of my blanket, I'd consider the good blessings I had: A soft pillow, a roof over my head, my husband next to me, and almost immediately I'd envision 40 days in the summer in a new and unfamiliar place each day, sleeping in a different hotel in a different town each night, and coming face-to-face with unforeseen challenges.

IIIIIIIIIIIIIIII

Many cyclists have pedaled across the United States, often doing so leisurely over three to nine months.

I had set myself a personal challenge of completing a 4,000-mile human-powered journey in 40 days.

This meant that even though my body would scream for me to stop pedaling and my motivation would fail, I couldn't stop. Even in the worst weather conditions, be it a torrential downpour or a hail storm, I couldn't stop to seek shelter and had to ride through it. Just so I could make the goal time.

Several people voiced their doubts about my ability to complete the ride. They were cyclists themselves, none of whom had attempted a cross-country ride.

"You are too ambitious. 100 miles a day is a lot to take for 40 days!" one said. "I've no doubt you'll begin this ride, but I doubt you'd be able to complete it," a close friend of mine announced in the presence of several others who had gathered at my send-off party a week before the ride.[2]

Whenever I had a really bad day and felt like giving up, I'd remember their words and would make sure I didn't let them win – I'd bite the bullet and keep on pedaling.

I learned that whatever you do, there will be those who support you and those who will never like you or agree with you, no matter how hard you try. You can't rally, excite, and inspire everybody. So if you can't sway your critics, move on. Don't focus your energy on them. It does you no good but it sure drains your enthusiasm. You'll be better off letting them go, focusing instead on those who support and care about what you do. If you take honest stock of the number of supporters versus the number of critics, you'll be surprised to find that there are more in the former camp than there are in the latter.

For every naysayer, I had many more positive and supportive friends. Every day on the road, people sent me messages and texts offering encouragement and prayers. My husband insisted that I never quit. He had invested too much of himself in supporting my dream.

So when the challenge became overwhelming, I could either quit and fly home or take it one pedal at a time, one

---

[2] It wasn't until two years later that I told him what he had said and he apologized profusely, saying he wasn't aware he had said that and he certainly didn't mean to doubt me. We are still friends today, and good friends at that.

day at a time. During those moments (which were frequent), I'd call to mind the bigger purpose behind the ride: I wanted to demonstrate that an ordinary girl like me, with my flaws, imperfections, and lack of better preparation, could do something great.

Every dream worth pursuing is worth being afraid of. Fear is not a bad thing. Fear was a useful ally because it made me tougher and enabled me to face what might taunt and intimidate others. I've learned to use my stubbornness and refusal to give up to my advantage. The more something intimidates me, the more I want to do it.

Kansas

On our last day in Colorado, some 60 miles before we would cross into Kansas, Derek offered some helpful information about his home state.

"Now, be warned. Kansas, a.k.a. Wheat Country, is flat as a pancake. No mountains like here [Colorado]. You can look in any direction and you can't see the end of it. It's that flat."

I didn't know what to imagine, so I imagined an airplane runway in a middle of a wheat field with grass as tall as ten feet.

"And windy all year. All day, everyday." He emphasized "everyday" to make sure I didn't miss it.

He went on, "It's wonderful, isn't it? To be that simple and boring at the same time. Flat and windy. Flat and windy. Nothing more, nothing less."

At that point, I must have looked confused, so Derek went in for the kill. "Trust me, Kansas is a great place to live. Now, why don't you call your husband and tell him to pack his bags because you're moving to Kansas? Life will be perfect."

I laughed then, but I would be far from laughing when we actually got to Kansas.

day 24 **Encounter: Woman at Casey's**

I had been rolling on the backroads of rural Kansas for 20 miles on a semi-flat tire. Thankfully it was a small puncture, enough for some air to be kept intact for several minutes. Every five miles or so, I'd stop to pump more air into the leaking tube.

After what seemed like a full day of work – cycling nimbly, avoiding rough road surfaces, stopping to put more air into the precarious tube every 20 minutes or so – we finally arrived in a small town with a big name, Scott City.

We headed straight for the main street, hoping to find a bicycle store. To our dismay, we found none. But we did spot a Casey's General Store, a large chain in the Midwest, and Derek suggested we head there for a break and see if we could fix the flat.

||||||||||||||||||

I came out of the bathroom. I saw a girl of about 14 first in line. Behind her was an older lady with shoulder-length blonde hair. They both looked very solemn. The girl's eyes were puffy. She had been crying and tears were welling in her eyes. The blonde lady lovingly put her arms around the crying teenager's shoulders and whispered into her ear. The teenager wiped away her tears with the back of her hands.

I went to the drink dispenser and filled up my empty water bottles.

"Are you a cyclist?" I turned around. It was the blonde lady in line outside the bathroom.

"Why, I thought so. I saw your bicycle outside the store and I suppose it belongs to you, seeing you're wearing cycling apparel."

"Yes, that's my bicycle outside."

"Are you racing across America?"

"Well, sort of. I'm cycling across America, and I'm racing to get there as fast as I can." I squirmed a little. I wasn't sure if I answered her question adequately.

"Oh my gosh!" she exclaimed. "You're racing across America? My husband and I have been tracking you guys!" She went on, "We are huge cycling fans. We cycled a lot together, and we love the Race Across America. We track the racers online every year. I can't believe I would meet an actual racer!"

"I'm not ..." I was about to explain that I wasn't racing in the Race Across America, when she said, "My husband died a week ago. I just buried him today."

"How ... how did he die?" I stammered. A bicycle accident, I thought in my head. "No, not bicycle," she replied, as if reading my mind, "but a freak motorcycle accident." She sighed. "He would have loved to meet a racer."

I stopped trying to explain myself, and instead, struggled to find the next comforting thing to say, when she looked at me, fighting back tears in her eyes, and asked, "Can I hug you?"

I was taken aback. "Yes, sure."

We hugged. Two strangers in a general store in the middle of Kansas.

We hugged for a long time. I held her tight. A stranger in my arms. A woman in grief.

When we let go of each other, she whispered in my ear, thank you, and walked out of the store. Outside, I saw her getting into a car with the teenager I had seen earlier.

I understood now why the teenager had been crying. She had just buried her father.

 — — — — — — — — — — — — — — — — — —

DAD

As a little boy, my dad dreamed of becoming a policeman. His father didn't think he had the right skills and never encouraged him. His family was so poor that all my father did was lots of housework, carrying logs and water pails and running errands for his extremely stern father.

He was often whipped mercilessly for coming home with dirt and blood stains on his school uniform from fights with older boys in school who teased him about the holes in his shoes and socks.

My father was so cruelly beaten by his dad that to this day, at age 73, he still occasionally dreams of his father beating the daylights out of him. I heard this recurring dream a few times during my childhood. It used to terrify my mom and me, because of the pain and agony I heard in his initially soft groans which progressively became louder until they became screams to stop hitting him.

My father is closest to me, perhaps because he saw similarities in us: We are both highly inquisitive and we are both fighters – we identify with strength, independence, rebellion and hard work.

Like my father, I have a fierce fighting spirit. I refuse to allow my circumstances to tell me what I can't do.

━━━ ━━━ ━━━ ━━━ ━━━ ━━━ ━━━ ━━━ ━━━ ━━━ ━━━ ━━━ ━━━ ━━━ ━━━ ━━━ ━━━

Kansas turned out to be exactly as Derek had described it.

Flat as a runway, there wasn't much climbing. While that was good news for our weary legs, flat terrains were also magnets for wind, because there really was nothing stopping winds from blowing through.

Because Kansas is just east of the Rocky Mountains, it's on the receiving end of high-pressure storm activities brewing in the mountains to the west.

Having just spent 21 days climbing the Rockies, riding in windy Kansas felt like we had just left the lion's den and entered a shark's jaw.

day 24 **Blow, Wind, Blow!**

As long as we were riding our bicycles, the wind kept blowing, head on, pushing us back with every knot. When we stopped to rest for the night, the wind stopped. It almost felt like nature was conspiring against us.

But strong winds weren't Kansas' only gift for us. She also gave us the hottest heat of summer. Cycling among those wheat fields was insanity and the wisest thing we could have done was stay indoors with the air-conditioning turned on full blast.

Each time we stopped to seek shelter from both the wind and heat, I'd wallow in despair and think, I can't do this any longer.

Derek was hurting too. It was written all over his face. He was no longer smiling or cracking jokes. He had lost the strength to cheer us up.

Occasionally I'd stop by the side of the road and scream out my frustration till my throat was hoarse. In the distance I'd hear another scream. It was Derek. He too, was letting off steam.

Other times I'd wail and howl like a hurting animal and plead with the wind to stop blowing, yet it wouldn't relent.

After two full days of nature's abuse, I broke down. I was crushed. While I had tried to encourage myself to pedal just one more mile when the going got tough, I lost the final ounce of willpower to keep going.

I texted my husband: "I'm having a mental breakdown. I'm taking the first flight home tomorrow."

day 26 **New Beginning**

I didn't buy the first ticket home.

Instead, I dropped out of the Trans America Bike Race.

||||||||||||||||

"I think I'm gonna quit this and go home to my parents' home when we get to Newton." His parents lived in El Dorado, some 40 miles from Newton. They had made plans to visit him when we rolled into Newton later in the day.

"But why?" I hadn't seen this coming.

"I'm running out of money. I only have several hundred dollars in the bank." He was almost sheepish at the mention of his bank balance.

"Don't worry, we'll share our food. We'll pull through!" I tried to convince him.

"I don't think I want to ride anymore. I'm done. I'm so near home. I think I'll just go home."

We were halfway across the country – how could he quit now? Yes, we both had been pretty beaten up by this stage of the trip. I myself was about to give up the previous night and somehow summoned new strength the next morning to keep going. I hadn't expected him to pull the plug this quickly.

I was deeply disappointed and didn't think I could persuade him otherwise. In my anger, I retorted, "Whatever," and sped off on my bicycle.

I rode by myself for the rest of the day. At lunch, Sam and Tom found me at a gas station having a bottle of orange juice and Lays potato chips. I was in no mood for proper food.

"Where's Derek?" Tom asked.

"He's quitting the ride."

"What? Are you serious?"

"I think he is."

"What are you gonna do?"

"I'm gonna have to ride without him."

"But Jason wouldn't let you," Sam reminded me.

He was right. My pact with my husband before the ride was that I would have a cycling buddy with me at all times.

||||||||||||||||

Evening rolled around. I finally reconnected with Derek at the Newton Bike Shop. "Hey Derek, sorry about this morning. I was mad because I felt abandoned by you."

"That's alright, I understand."

"Erm, we have a suggestion – Sam, Tom and I. Care to hear us out?"

We stated our case. Up to that point, none of us had enjoyed the journey. The towns had been small and spread far apart. We constantly lost cell phone communication in the mountains. Sam and Tom would wait for hours in between towns. We each needed something new to motivate us to keep going.

Besides, the upcoming states on the Trans America Bike Trail promised more arduous hill climbs. Climbing more hills would push back the completion date and stretch our depleting funds. We couldn't afford it.

We decided that the best way forward would be quit the race and create a new route east. A route that would avoid the steep Appalachian Mountains in Virginia and West Virginia so we could complete the ride to the east coast in the next 13 days. A new route that would have us passing through bigger and more exciting towns.

Derek listened quietly. He was reluctant at first, but soon relented. He agreed to quit the Trans America Bike Race and continue riding east with me on a new route.

I will be forever grateful to Derek for his flexibility and unwavering support when I needed him.

day 28 **Eastbound**

As we rode towards Missouri, we noticed that the wind had died down. Finally, I thought. Throwing the affliction of the previous days behind me, I re-fixed my focus on the road, anticipating our final destination.

Some 20 miles before the Kansas-Missouri state line, we rode past a decent-sized town, Paolo, and started noticing some hills, which was a welcome relief after several days of extreme flatness.

Ironically, while I was laboring up steep passes in the Rocky Mountains, I wished for the flat plains of Kansas; yet after several days of the flattest terrain whichever way the eye looked, I yearned for mountain climbs.

It's incredible how short our memory of physical pain can be. It's almost as if there was an invisible reset button: one moment we're hurting and wanting out; the next moment we're out (of pain) and wanting the next challenge.

Perhaps that is the essence of the human spirit – we adapt to changing situations quickly.

Crew Management

When you're out on a long stretch of road with no one in sight among mountains, trees, rivers; and more mountains, trees, and rivers, the sound of an approaching vehicle can be rather exciting. I might have been fooling myself into believing that I had some sort of psychic power, but I could almost swear when I heard the soft hum of a vehicle approaching behind us, it had to be Sam and Tom. And I was right.

I expected them to show up at least once during the day, so I was riding with heightened anticipation.

Derek and I were secretly delighted when a camera started pointing at our faces as we rode. Such a relief to see familiar faces! Sometimes, where there weren't other vehicles on the road, Sam and Tom would drive alongside Derek and me, and the four of us would spout nonsense or crack silly jokes and riddles. Here's one:

What did the dog say when its master rubbed sandpaper on its bottom? Rough, rough!

While Derek and I were constant physical pain, Sam and Tom weren't exactly having a field day either.

Tom drove while Sam filmed. It was a partnership that worked well. They had been working on video filming, editing, and animation projects for several years before jumping on this adventure with me.

Phone signals were sketchy and often unreliable. Tracking me down was a sort of cat and mouse game. The only clue as to my whereabouts was emitted by a GPS tracker strapped onto my bike. In between erratic phone signals, they'd verify my exact location on www.trackleaders.com (a web application that tracks adventure races in the United States).

They would be waiting at a spot expecting me to show up so they could film me. While it takes a vehicle a half hour to get to a town 30 miles away, it takes a bicycle two hours on a flat or downhill route, or 2.5 hours on a steep route. Including food or bathroom breaks, we could reach Sam and Tom up to three hours later.

Sam and Tom had expected an epic and beautiful American adventure; they were not expecting the same thing, over and over, day in and day out. We would very often lose phone signals in the mountains or deep in the woods; they'd lose track of us and tried hard to hunt Derek and me down for up to six hours a day.

This happened every day for six weeks and was understandably frustrating for them.

|||||||||||||||

I had underestimated the enormity of the tasks on my plate: Ride my bicycle, lead the team, and direct the shots for the film. I had thought I could manage them all without any problem, given the cycling time was what I estimated to be between six and eight hours a day. With 24 hours in a day, surely I would be able to juggle my role well without a hitch.

Oh how naive I was!

I was so physically exhausted from the daily battle of completing the determined mileage before dark that I didn't have the capacity to manage a camera crew. I couldn't direct the shoot scenes and cycle at the same time. I could only focus on one thing, which was to pedal.

I couldn't nourish my body sufficiently for the physical demands I made of it. We ate whatever was available at rest stops, which in most cases meant simple sugar and processed food from gas stations, convenience stores, or fast food joints.

Consumed by my own struggles, I neglected the feelings and interests of my camera crew. They had wanted to get their job done well, but my frequent tardiness in arriving at designated meeting points resulted in their waiting in the vehicle for hours, with little to do.

I was eager to have a happy crew, and I wanted us to have a good working relationship, so I would try my best to cycle as quickly as I could, often pushing myself harder than I should have.

By the second week, I was frustrated that we hadn't had any interviews with people on film. Derek and I had stopped for breakfast in a convenience store in Montana that turned out to be a cafe with a backroom full of casino machines. I saw several elderly men wearing cowboy hats having burritos for breakfast, and a lone man at a slot machine. I almost wished I could wrangle a story out of them, just so I could have an interview on film, and hoped that miraculously, their story might be an interesting one: Perhaps the man at the slot machine was once a millionaire who owned huge acres of cattle grazing land. Maybe his son died mysteriously of a strange, degenerative disease, his wife went insane and soon after died. In his loneliness, he turned to the dark world of gambling, which sucked him into a slow, slippery descent to losing his entire fortune. Now broke and a little insane, he tries his hand at slot machines, wistfully trying to recoup his losses, a dollar at a time.

But these stories couldn't be made up – we were filming a documentary, not a Hollywood movie.

The creative direction of the film had not gone according to plan and I must have projected my frustration onto my team.

||||||||||||||||||

Despite their disappointment with the job they had signed up for and my lack of tact in my spoken communication with them, Sam and Tom conducted themselves professionally and continued to gather footage for the film, while I kept riding east.

A day after the ride ended in Baltimore, we drove to New York City as we had made plans to fly out of the JFK airport to our respective destinations.

When we parted ways in New York, we did so amicably and promised that the next phase in our working relationship would be much smoother – we would have the documentary edited and completed several months later. It would be a rather straightforward process. We did not anticipate further problems.

Unfortunately, the second phase of our working relationship took a turn for the worse, and I was largely to blame.

▲ Missouri River, the longest
river in the United States at
approximately 2,341 miles.

Midwest

day 28 Missouri

Missouri is often mocked as "misery." Pretty clever pun. I was fortunate to experience anything but misery.

The minute we crossed into Missouri, I noticed the grass was green, the sky was clear and blue, the birds were chirping. I knew that the ride from hereon would be beautiful, and it was.

Day Two in Missouri, we rode across the Missouri River and stopped, entranced by the peace and tranquility of the water beneath us. I leaned my bike on the bridge, took a photo of it, and lingered a minute longer, simply taking in the beauty of the moment.

day 31 Encounter: Greg Griffin

That's weird, I thought. Why is he wheeling himself on my side of the road?

The man had a long beard and dark shades, and kept his eyes on the ground as his hands firmly gripped and turned the wheels.

I watched the gap between us narrow as we approached

each other from opposite directions, on the same road shoulder.

As he came closer, I stopped. "If you don't mind me asking, why do you wheel yourself on this side of the road?"

"So I can see who knocks me down," he replied matter-of-factly. I was dumbfounded. He intrigued me even more now.

"Where are you headed?" I asked, trying to get him to talk some more. I had a feeling he had quite a story.

"To the store a mile down the road to buy beer and cigarettes."

He was about to keep going when I decided it was an ask-now-or-never moment.

"I know I just met you, and I don't mean to come across as rude or insensitive, but would you tell me what happened to your legs?" I was trying my utmost to be as gentle as I could with a question as fragile as that.

"Oh no, not at all. I was involved in an accident. Several years ago."

A bassist in a rock band, he was drinking beer with his pals on a bridge one night when a group of men approached and picked a fight with them. In the scuffle, one of the men got in his car, reversed and ran straight into Greg, pinning him to the wall of the bridge. Greg's spine was severely injured.

He underwent several surgeries and was hospitalized for six months. Paralyzed from the waist down and told by his doctor that he would never walk again, he plunged into depression. He would yell at his band mates who came to visit and antagonize them for saving his life, saying he'd rather be dead than a cripple.

To alleviate his pain, Greg supplemented the doctor-prescribed morphine with his own supply. After his discharge from the hospital, Greg's life spun out of control. His dependency on morphine increased. Unable to finance his habit or provide for his mother and his young son, he became a drug dealer. He was caught and put through a rehabilitation program. Upon his release, he was back in business.

He lived in constant fear of the danger he was putting his family in because of his drug dealing. After a near-death confrontation outside his home, a drug deal that went sour, he decided to sever ties with the underworld and checked himself into a drug rehabilitation program.

He eventually met a girl who loved him and encouraged him to lead a clean life. Several years of rehabilitation and a number of relapses later, he finally pulled through. When I met him, he had been sober for two years.

That's not all there is to Greg's story.

One night, while drinking and playing pool with his pals, he saw a man walk into the bar. He recognized him instantly as the man who ran his car into him and left him for dead. At that point, Greg had a revolver in his pocket. He wrapped his hand around the revolver, gripped it tight, and contemplated putting a bullet through the man's head. He thought of his son and mother. He thought of his girlfriend. He had a complete family now. People who loved him. People who stood by him through his darkest

moments. It would be selfish of him to seek revenge and hurt his family by going to prison. He had worked so hard to sober up and rebuild his life. The revenge wasn't worth him throwing his life away.

He released his grip on the revolver and walked away. He never saw the man again.

I almost teared up when I heard his story. "What do you do now, Greg?"

"Oh I just live day by day, making the best of each day. I can't work because of my paralysis, and I am on social welfare, but I do my best to love my family and be there for them. I had dreams of being a Marine but that's not possible now. That's alright. I'm back to playing bass and making music with my pals. Life is good."

"How do you view this lot you've been dealt with in life?" I was trying to tread lightly.

"I see it this way: If someone, a young person perhaps, can learn something out of what I have been through, it will have been worth it. If your life sucks and you're thinking of suicide, don't. If you persevere and believe in God, you will pull through. There is hope for tomorrow. Look at me. I am living proof of that."

day 35 Jackson, Ohio

No larger than a man's fist, the balled up dark substances were starting to appear more and more frequently on road shoulders. In fact, they were starting to form a sequence of sorts – every mile or two, there'd be several of them, followed by a mile or two of clean road, and then the lumps would appear again. This went on for several miles.

After a while, I turned to Derek, "Say, that looks like horse poo, don't you think?" "Yeah," was Derek's simple reply. He was equally puzzled by the lumps we had to dodge from time to time, but they were a distraction from the endlessly long and straight road.

As I contemplated the bizarre thought of a horse allowed on a freeway, I caught sight of a trotting creature on the other side of the road.

I thought the rising humidity and afternoon sun must have blinded me to the point of hallucination, but as the creature drew closer, still on the other side of the road, I realized I wasn't hallucinating – it was an actual horse drawing a wooden carriage.

It then dawned on me it was an Amish family riding an open-top horse carriage! An Amish family! I had heard that there was a sizable Amish community in Ohio and I had wanted to meet and chat with one, so imagine my joy when we actually did chance upon one.

"Derek, let's turn around!" In my excitement, I forgot my road manners and did not look out for oncoming vehicles before getting out of the bike lane. I would have been hit by a semi-truck traveling at full speed had Derek not shouted at me to stop in time.

Thank God for Derek.

Once we crossed to the other side of the road, we quickly gave chase. The horse was trotting at about 10 mph so it wasn't long before we caught up to it. I thought horses were capable of much higher speeds? It must have considered its passengers' safety to trod along so slowly. What a sweet creature.

The carriage had wooden wheels, and not rubber tires as vehicles do. At the helm of the carriage was a fully bearded man with a strange-looking tall hat and a two-piece black and white suit. A full suit in the middle of summer! Seated next to him was presumably his wife. She was dressed in a long black dress with white trimmings, and a matching white cap. Their teenage daughter sat in the back.

We pedaled quietly behind the horse, not chatting with each other as we didn't want to startle either the horse or the family. We didn't try to make ourselves invisible either – that would not have been possible. We were plainly visible and pedaled as if we were not tailing them but traveling in the same direction.

Every so often, the couple's daughter would turn around to look at us. She did it so frequently it made her mother, seated at the front, also turn around. The mother must have communicated that to the father, who later on, also turned around to check out what the fuss was all about.

They told us there are some 40 families living in their little community in Jackson, Ohio.

It was typical for the family to ride their horse carriage 10 miles downtown to buy groceries.

Just last week, they attended their older daughter's wedding in Pennsylvania. "Did you ride the carriage?" I asked. Pennsylvania was at least 200 miles away.

Surely the poor horse wouldn't be able to sustain the distance. "No, no, we didn't. We took a car."

"But pardon me, I thought you don't drive?"

"Oh we got a ride from a friend. If we have to travel farther than 20 miles, we catch a ride. If it's nearby, we ride our carriage."

Our conversation was starting to turn friendly when the carriage driver spotted a flashing red light coming from Derek's GoPro camera attached to his helmet.

"Excuse us, we gotta be on our way," he said suddenly.

"Oh sure, thanks for chatting with us. It's really nice meeting you," I said to him and his wife.

The family rode off, leaving a trail of dust behind them. Their daughter turned back one last time to wave goodbye.

I thought she looked sad that they had to leave. She looked like she wanted to chat. I had wanted to chat longer too.

Between Towns

Cycling across a country, let alone a continent, is a cool idea, until you're actually on the road and you realize how vast the land is, how long the roads are and how terribly lonely it gets.

I was fortunate that I had a cycling buddy for the entire ride. We hit it off easily, as we are both pretty easy going – more so Derek, as I was the one constantly setting goals for waking up, setting off, distance to cover for the day, and length of each rest stop.

Derek and I looked forward to arriving at the next town, because that meant rest, a chance to stand or rest our butts on something other than our bicycle saddles, grab some food, top up our water bottles and use the port-a-potty, or a proper restroom if we were lucky, and sometimes, we even had the opportunity to chat with another human being.

ııııııııııııııı

How did we know we were approaching a town? The signs were rather obvious:

Gas stations. From a mile away, we'd see signs of a gas station. More often that not, gas stations set up shop either at highway intersections or in areas where there are other amenities, like convenience stores or restaurants.

Derek is a good storyteller. He fueled 90% of the conversation, sharing stories of his life with doses of philosophy and quick-witted humor. But when we saw signs of an approaching town and I was on the verge of bonking (running out of fuel to cycle further), I'd interrupt him in the middle of his stories and yell, "gas station!" and pedal as fast as I could, racing him to get there first.

Speed limit signs. As we were riding mostly on local highways with speed limits of 55-60 mph, whenever we saw signs that said "slow down" or "reduce speed now" or "speed limit 35 mph," we would perk up, finding new strength to pedal quicker for a mile or two until we rolled into town.

Water towers. This is especially true in the Midwest. These are usually round, shaped like a lollipop, and approximately 130 feet tall, with the town name or some form of abbreviation inscribed on the side, visible from several miles away.

Food

America is a land of culinary diversity, isn't it? I had this grandiose idea that I would be savoring great food throughout my ride. I mean, why wouldn't I make that assumption? In previous trips driving from city to city and state to state, I had the luxury of enjoying different offerings in different cities.

I had the most appetizing spread of Mexican delights in California; the best BBQ ribs and the softest and fluffiest dinner rolls served with melted cinnamon and honey butter in North Carolina, and of course, the thinnest yet most satisfying piece of pizza in the Big Apple, just to name a few. Of course, in between those stops, I had mostly fast and convenient food from drive-thrus and gas stations, but I must have forgotten this little but important fact when I planned for my ride.

I envisioned getting into town for a good plate of lunch, and at the end of the day, I'd check into a motel, shower, and present myself clean in a restaurant for dinner deserving of a 100-mile ride. I even went so far as to prepare a spreadsheet of miles I expected to log in a day, with lunch and dinner stops along the way and available restaurants in those towns, relying on Yelp and TripAdvisor for restaurant reviews and tips.

I later found out, while on the road, that 98% of my research was wasted. I did not stop at the towns as I had planned. Instead, we would fuel ourselves with whatever we could find in a gas station, and that often meant peanut butter crackers, muffins, croissants, and pizza slices.

Or we would be grinding uphill in a national park amidst great beauty and remoteness but not having eaten anything

▲ Best pancakes ever,
found at John Day, Oregon.

▲ Asian noodles at Athens, Ohio.

▲ Pasta at McKenzie River Bridge, Oregon.

▲ Soft dinner rolls with cinnamon butter at Walden, Colorado.

for more than three hours, we were faint with hunger and despite our most valiant efforts to pedal as fast as our legs would turn over quickly enough, by the time we got into the nearest town, we were a half hour too late – the restaurants were all closed for their mid-day break. No!

We would look forward to getting into the next small town, only to discover that the town had a population of ten, with more chickens and cattle than humans. It was supposed to have a population of ten, but where were the humans? We'd see no one – perhaps the heat of summer drove them indoors, peering at us dust-clad cyclists from their windows.

Sometimes the distance from one town to another was 50 miles, which took three to four hours to get to, depending on how flat or steep the road was.

We'd spot some sign of civilization, but with just a few pedals, we'd be rolling out of town. The town only had two houses.

This happened frequently, sometimes several times in a day, and especially so in Kansas, where the towns are small and deserted. On Sundays, gas stations were closed while church parking lots were full.

Note to cyclists passing through the Bible Belt states on Sundays: make sure you're stocked up with water and food because you'll be hard pressed to find a store open on the Lord's day.

After two weeks of such frequent despair, we finally learned to manage our expectations and would stock up on as much water and food as possible for each day. We didn't want to injure our broken spirits further in desolate towns.

Food Cravings

Our food cravings changed from week to week. The first week, we craved peanut butter stuffed Ritz crackers and got them from every store we walked into. The second week, we craved gummy bears, because we needed sugar in our systems to give us the extra boost when our bodies and legs were growing weary. The third week, we craved apples and would grab them at breakfast from the motels we stayed in. The fourth week, we craved cream cheese and egg croissant sandwiches.

Yet at every dinner stop I noticed a strange thing: my body craved salad. You would think that after a full day of cycling the body would crave carbohydrates like sandwiches, pastries, rice and noodles. But no, I craved salad. I think it was my body's way of trying to reverse the effect of all the sugar I was eating.

I had pancakes almost every morning. Our routine was to have a bite or two of a cheap, cold bagel from the motel before we set off at 6:00 a.m. and cycle until we spotted the nearest town with a decent breakfast cafe, where I'd order two pancakes and a side of eggs for protein, plus coffee with refills. Derek would usually order a breakfast burrito or a big breakfast of bacon, eggs, and potatoes, and his standard cup of O.J., which I later found out, stood for orange juice.

Best Meals

Pancakes and coffee. I couldn't do without either in the morning or else I'd be grumpy and unhappy until I got them. I had the yummiest pancakes on Day Four in the town of John Day in Oregon. The pancakes were so delightful I think I might make a trip to John Day again just for those pancakes.

▲ A cup of joe is crucial for a happy morning.

They were bigger than my face, tenderly fluffy, blueberry flavored, and tasted oh so good.

The best food I dug into was a most delicious plate of penne pasta with blackened chicken at McKenzie River Bridge, Oregon on the second day of the ride. We had been exhausted from riding 150 miles on the first day and 130 miles on the second day until we got to McKenzie River Bridge late in the evening. Imagine our pleasant surprise to find a restaurant across the street from the motel. We went over and placed our order just before the kitchen closed for the night. I rarely eat pasta, but that plate was so delightful it still makes me smile when I think about it.

Also, who would have thought that a small mosquito-infested town called Walden in the middle of Colorado would serve amazing steak and soft dinner rolls with silky smooth cinnamon butter which reminded me of those I had had in North Carolina on a previous road trip?

So smitten were we with the dinner rolls and cinnamon butter that we politely asked if the restaurant might give us free helpings of the rolls, as most restaurants would, but they refused, so we made order after order for those tiny soft rolls at $1.50 a piece – a high profit for a restaurant in the middle of nowhere, if you ask me!

In the college town of Athens, Ohio, we spotted an Asian noodle shop. I was delighted! Asian food was hard to come by during our ride. I had *pad thai*; Derek had Taiwanese noodles. They were not authentic, my sensitive Asian taste buds told me, but we were famished and enjoyed the rare treat.

Weather

I didn't know that it could snow or hail in the summer, but it did in Montana.

Or that the weather at high altitudes could switch so suddenly and precariously (much like a woman's mood – I can say that because I'm a woman), as it did at Yellowstone and the Rocky Mountains and in Montana, Wyoming, and Colorado.

Or that the winds in Kansas could be so strong, violent, and persistent and always seem to blow from the direction you were heading.

Or that threatening dark clouds, flashes of lightning, and thunderstorms could roll in all at once into Missouri and Illinois without warning, transforming an otherwise sunny and humid day into a miserable day of heavy downpours.

Or that sirens of tornado warnings go off mid-morning or mid-afternoon in Ohio and Indiana like it's a daily occurrence (fortunately we didn't run into any!).

I could deal with the physical pain of consecutive-day steep mountain passes – I resorted to painkillers. I could even deal with the heat – when temperatures soared to the high nineties and I felt like a watermelon about to explode, I sought shelter in shaded areas or drank water by the gallon like a camel.

But I was not prepared for the extreme cold at high altitudes. I researched town, hotel, and food stops but not the weather. How was I, a tropical girl from Southeast Asia, and more recently in sunny California, to know that snow was common in the summer in certain parts of the United States?

Naively, I brought only summer cycling attire. I had two thin long sleeved jackets, a pair of arm warmers and legs warmers, which, all combined, could barely retain any body heat or provide insulation against the assault of the snow and rain.

Someone once told me, it's not about the weather, it's about having the right attire. I wish I had met that someone before the trip.

West Virginia

day 36 Despair

I was excited to cross into West Virginia, the second to last state. It would only be another 400 miles to the east coast and the end of the ride. I grew up with a baby boomer mom who listened to the records of the day, particularly John Denver's famous hit, "Country Roads", and chided myself for mistaking "mountains mama" in the song for "country mama," thinking that the state would be welcomingly beautiful with lustrous green pasture, a land overflowing with milk and honey. Despite my lack of research, I had some inkling that the Appalachian Mountains covered most of Virginia and West Virginia, but having ridden the Rocky Mountains, I naively thought to myself, how bad could the Appalachians be?

Besides, we had intentionally planned our route to skirt north of the Appalachians to avoid climbing its treacherous hills. The towns on our route included Parkersburg, Ellensboro, Clarksburg, Grafton, Aurora, New Creek, and Romney.

We rode half the state on Highway 50, next to large trucks and semis that threatened to run us over if we tried to steer even a little out of the right shoulder that wasn't meant to be a cycling lane.

Roadkill was a common sight along Highway 50. We saw untold amounts of dead meat on the road shoulder.

Two questions popped into my head as I focused hard to avoid running over the carcasses:

What's the driving culture of West Virginia? Are the drivers maniacs who love the sound of thud and sight of blood, or are the creatures of the field so attracted to the sounds of zooming traffic, speeding cars, loud truck horns, and roaring motorcycles that they charge blindly into oncoming vehicles only to be knocked dead on the spot?

And what's with the debris on the road shoulders? It was as if some dude had driven his construction truck slowly along the highway and scattered pieces of debris on the road shoulder, on purpose. There were little stones, some smooth and some jagged; scattered mounds of dark-colored, almost blackish sand; occasionally some broken pieces of glass; and not uncommonly, a nail or two.

As you can imagine, it was the furthest thing from a smooth ride. Derek and I rode nimbly to avoid tire punctures while trying to quicken our pace because the vehicles on our left were zooming past so swiftly we felt like we had to try our best to match their speed. The sounds of rushing traffic were deafening.

As we rode into Bridgeport from Clarksburg to stay the night as the last light of day gave way to night, a feeling of dread swept over us. Houses with peeling paint, shattered glass windows, and falling roofs. Shreds of waste and rubbish strewn on the front lawns of houses, often spilling onto the rail tracks. Laundry put out to dry on porch railings or clotheslines in the yard. Occasionally you'd spot men smoking cigarettes, their singlets revealing pot bellies and oversized dirty pants held up by broken belts.

Our motel was in a depressing state. The ceiling of the room was literally falling off. The bathroom had yellow stains in the tub. The bed sheets were thin from repeated use and wash. An unpleasant odor permeated the room. Our neighbors in the motel were blue-collar men, many of them shirtless, cigarette in one hand and beer bottle in the other. I didn't ask, but assumed they worked in construction, given their outfits, rough manners and mud-slabbed trucks in the parking lot.

We slept little and got out of town at the crack of dawn. We pressed east.

As we rode towards Virginia, well-paved roads eventually gave way to pot-holed steep, winding roads.

While the climbs in the Rocky Mountains averaged an 8% gradient, the Appalachians averaged 11%. What's a 3% difference, you ask? To a cyclist – it means a whole lot! The Climbing Cyclist (www.theclimbingcyclist.com) explains:

- 0%: A flat road.
- 1-3%: Slightly uphill but not particularly challenging. A bit like riding into the wind.
- 4-6%: A manageable gradient that can cause fatigue over long periods.
- 7-9%: Starting to become uncomfortable for seasoned riders, and very challenging for new climbers.

- 10%-15%: A painful gradient, especially if maintained for any length of time.
- 16%+: Very challenging for riders of all abilities. Maintaining this sort of incline for any length of time is very painful.

The Appalachian Mountains in West Virginia fall within the second hardest category. To put it simply, it was highly discomforting; almost to the point of excruciating muscle burn, especially when the climb extends more than three miles.

My breath became short and labored while my leg muscles screamed in agony with every pedal. Derek and I kept going. We stopped talking to each other altogether as we focused on climbing.

We could almost smell the salty air of the east coast. There was no stopping now.

Windmills of My Mind

What did I think about while cycling so many hours a day? Lots. These were some of my thoughts, which turns out, were lessons I learned on the ride:

I need little in life

When you reduce your life to basic necessities, life becomes really simple.

Who would have thought that you could carry all you need for 39 days on a bicycle? No need for a car, house, furniture, or material possessions except whatever is necessary to live day by day on the road.

The simpler life is, the easier it is to be present and to be in the moment.

The more things we own, the more we care for them – that makes us focus on material things, which don't last, while the more important things, like people and relationships get pushed to second place.

We don't need a lot of food either – we eat far more than what our bodies need to function.

I don't need the right time to do the right thing

There is no perfect season to pursue your dream. I set my heart on a goal and went after it.

Were there challenges and difficulties? Yes. Plenty.

I wanted to cycle across the country, but wasn't an endurance cyclist, so I found a coach to train me. I needed financing for the ride so I wrote to various companies for sponsorship and appealed to my community for contributions.

Were the conditions perfect? No.

The weather derailed my progress but I dug my heels in and kept pedaling forward.

I didn't wait until I had everything in order. I took steps forward and the path ahead started revealing itself.

It is safe to travel across the country

Save for a few people who tried to run Derek and me off the road or hollered vulgarities at us in Oregon and Indiana, the people I met on the road were angels in disguise.

Like James Barringer, who owns a bike shop in Newton,

Kansas, a midway point in the cross country ride. A few days before our arrival in town (he had been tracking our progress via www.trackleaders.com), he asked us what we would like to eat, and prepared exactly that. Ok, he didn't smoke the ribs himself but he sure ordered it from the best restaurant in town! They were the best ribs I have ever eaten. The meat was perfectly cooked, tastefully seasoned, and fell off the bones. He also checked both our bikes and made sure that all the parts and components were tuned and in good condition to take on the second half of the journey.

Derek spent a night in his parents' home not too far from James' shop. I stayed in the bike shop – there was a backroom for passing cyclists to sleep in, but there was no shower. James went out of his way for a total stranger, a dirty, smelly and soiled cyclist, by giving me a ride to his house so I could take a nice, hot shower and get cleaned up.

I have been a fortunate beneficiary of many people's kindness and while I can't possibly repay them, I will find a way to pay it forward in one way or another.

I did too much research

I spent a huge amount of time researching which motels to stop at and the kinds of food available along the bike route, but when I was on the road, I barely used that information at all. I didn't end up staying in the towns and motels I had planned on, simply because the physical exhaustion and weather threw curve balls.

For instance, I had planned to stop at mile 120 on the first day. It turned out to be a little residential town with only a grocery store at an intersection. There wasn't a place to put up for the night, so we had to cycle 16 miles to the next town, which was a casino resort town. I thought, great, surely there would be rooms in a casino hotel. As luck would have it, it was a Saturday, that hotel was the only one in town, and it was filled with locals and visitors excited to spend the weekend gambling. There was not a room to be had, despite our most sincere pleas. I must admit we looked rather disheveled and the posh hotel was doubtful we could pay for a night's stay.

Dejected, we had to cycle until we found a small bed and breakfast. On my lead, four of us (we had been a small party of cyclists: Derek; Ling, a friend from Singapore who eventually completed a fourth of the entire trip with us; Joe, a Spanish cyclist who was riding by himself; and me) rode towards the B&B, but after several miles of not seeing the B&B where it should be, I realized we had cycled in the wrong direction! We had to turn back and pedal extra miles to where we made a wrong turn. Almost driven mad with hunger, we stopped at a gas station for microwaveable pasta with meat sauce (which took forever to warm up – gas stations don't provide the highest wattage microwaves), which tasted heavenly in such dire conditions. After having our fill and layering up as the night was getting cold, we cycled, in the right direction this time, to the B&B.

Derek and I were racing each other ahead, and after a while, we noticed that Ling and Joe weren't behind us. We waited, fixing our gaze at the road, hoping to catch glimpses of their blinking headlights. Nothing. Five minutes went by. Then ten minutes. We were exhausted and reluctant to cycle any more than necessary so we waited some more. Finally, after waiting about 15 minutes in the cold, we decided something was very wrong and that we should turn back to look for them.

We didn't get very far before spotting them on the side of the road, fixing a flat tire in the dark.

The flat fixed, the four of us finally rode on and made it to the B&B, which cost us twice what we would pay for a cheap motel, but we gladly split the cost, took turns to shower and slept like babies on that first night.

Steaming hot coffee, homemade bacon, omelettes and toast would be served the next morning at 9:00 a.m., but we couldn't wait until after breakfast to hit the road. We woke up at 5:00 a.m. and took off at 6:00 a.m. Another long day beckoned.

Because the mileage on Day One was extended, our accommodation plans for the second and subsequent nights were disrupted. It was unrealistic and unnecessary of me to put in all that time and effort into researching towns and restaurants because plans changed while on the move.

It would however have been helpful to have had a rough idea of what each town we would be riding through had to offer. Information like population size, because that tells a lot – a small town of under 100 people is unlikely to have a hotel.

In the future, I thought to myself, I would equip myself with more knowledge of what to expect every 10-20 miles on the road: Are there gas stations for water and snacks? Do those towns have grocery stores or cafes? Cyclists are always looking for cheap and quick food alternatives that aren't typical fast food.

Unlikely Candidate

I don't like dirt on my stuff. I wipe my belongings clean after every use. When I bought my first $2,000 bicycle in 2010, a Scott Contessa CR1 Team, I'd prop it up on a bicycle stand after each ride and gingerly wipe off every particle of dirt with a piece of cloth and a dab of liquid soap.

I have since owned more bikes, but never more than one at a time. Before each new bike purchase, I'd sell the former. I've always been a minimalist that way and never quite understood the need for more than one bike. Many cyclists, I've noticed, own several bikes, each serving different purposes and terrains: a road bike for paved roads; a mountain bike for off roads, trails, or gravel; a commuter bike for getting around the city or to and from the convenience store; and possibly a beat-up bike for commuting in a city like San Francisco where the chances of having your bike stolen are almost, sad to say, a hundred percent.

My latest pride and joy is a Cannondale CAAD10, which I've owned since May 2012. It has seen the better part of California and America these past 3.5 years, but it looks as new as when I first laid eyes on it in a bike store in Palo Alto. The CAAD10 is arguably the stiffest and best performing aluminum bike, worth every penny I paid for it. Not only is it a thousand dollars cheaper than a carbon bike, it is durable, reliable, and has withstood several years of extensive use.

I don't like mess. I keep my belongings tidy and neatly arranged, no matter where I go, even in a hotel room or during an outdoor camping trip. I don't let my stuff lie around the house. Every item goes back to where it belongs. I take dirt, grease, and grime very seriously and get rid of it as soon as I spot it.

I don't like the cold. I'd much prefer to stay indoors when the weather outside looks the least bit threatening. California does have its imperfect days, especially near the Pacific Ocean, and the Bay Area where I live is often shrouded in a cold, gloomy fog and ever so frequently on the receiving end of cold coastal winds that makes a day out without a jacket a self-sabotaging idea.

Contrary to the conventional image you might have of an adventurer – someone strong, tough, rugged, and able to rough and tumble with the elements, whatever nature threw at him or her along the way – I don't fit that description.

Besides, I am not the fittest or fastest cyclist there is. How then did I manage to cycle across the third largest country in the world?

I realized that we don't have to be perfect to pursue our dreams. While I lacked the qualities associated with an ultra distance endurance cyclist, I made up for it with an indomitable will.

A moment of stillness upon arrival ▶
in Baltimore, Maryland.

▲ A victorious end to the journey
across a continent.

Maryland

Growing up in a lower middle class family, I was taught frugality was a virtue, chided for indulging in luxury, and until my adulthood, lived very simply. I've always found great joy in whatever I have at each moment. Sometimes I smile in the middle of a walk, reflecting on the amazing blessings I have – a brain that functions well, an inquisitive mind, air in my lungs, limbs that work, a healthy body. What more can I ask for? Would riches make me any happier? Perhaps riches can buy me things that I could only look at with envy through a store window (a shiny, brand new road bike, for instance), but they wouldn't make my heart any fuller than what it is already filled with – gratitude.

I had little in the bank but was full of joy when I pedaled to Inner Harbor in Baltimore, got off my bike, and concluded a 4,000-mile, 39-day journey.

My mind was blank. I was calm and at peace, almost zen-like. The previous weeks of rushing to this point has ended.

I spoke to the camera for the last time, reflecting on the journey. The camera crew, Derek, and I had dinner near the budget hotel we checked into, and went to bed the same time as we usually did.

Yes, it was as unceremonious as that.

A simple conclusion to a big bike ride. The way I liked it.

IIIIIIIIIIIIIII

I woke up the next morning as I had the past many mornings, at 5:00 a.m.

Wait a minute, I thought, I don't have to wake up this early anymore. The ride is over. I don't need to pedal anymore.

Post Ride

Somehow I wasn't on cloud nine when I completed the ride. It wasn't that I didn't want it to end; rather, I felt a pang of nostalgia, a tinge of sadness that I would be going back to a predictable life.

According to American travel writer and novelist Paul Theroux in *The Tao of Travel*, "In the pathology of travel, many journeyers who seem in pursuit of a goal are driven by demons, attempting to flee, often unsuccessfully, some condition of the mind." Theroux further quoted British scholar and explorer Sir Richard Burton: "Travelers, like poets, are mostly an angry race."

I liked being pushed to the edge and having to dig deep within myself to produce that which I didn't know I had.

While I was on the road, I was constantly on the defensive and had to look out for bigger, faster vehicles, nasty road conditions, and capricious weather. When I got home, it felt disconcerting to be surrounded by so many luxuries. I had to re-adapt and re-learn how to live as I did before. My first day back in the car felt strange. Life shouldn't be this comfortable,

I thought to myself.

Life on the road kept me humble and simple. I was acutely aware of my own mortality. I was thankful daily that I was protected from harm. I controlled what I could (mostly food), and adapted to what I couldn't (mostly weather). Nature was my playground and I played by her rules.

It took many months for me to settle down back home, and even after I did, I struggled with a deep yearning for a life back on the road. I would go out on bike rides, but riding the local routes just didn't feel the same anymore. I had been on longer, farther roads that brought me across towns, cities, and states, not to mention an entire country! The same activities, sights, and terrain at home no longer held their appeal.

I like simplicities in life. I often mused to myself – just give me my running shoes, bicycle, MacBook, camera, and coffee, and I would be a very happy gal. Give me anything more – a house, a car, furniture, more clothes – and they weigh me down like a ton of bricks. I feel suffocated by possessions. This probably explains why several weeks on the road thrills me so. Yet I can't be nomadic all the time – I have to be present for my husband, family, friends, and community. It's a fine line to tread, and I don't think I have quite mastered it.

Commitment

How do I say this without bursting anyone's balloon? I don't like cycling.

Before you stone me and claim me a fraud ("What? How can someone who doesn't like cycling cycle across America?"), please hear me out.

I'm telling you this because it takes more than just passion to realize a dream. I think passion is overrated. Yes, passion can get you motivated and started, but ultimately, what's going to see you through the rough spots and challenges is commitment.

Contrary to popular belief that passion is instrumental in achieving goals, I'd like to submit that commitment is even more important.

Commitment is that single focus on the goal, in the presence or absence of passion. Commitment is the engine that drives you towards your dream.

Commitment was what got me to the finish line when I had neither the motivation nor passion to keep going.

Focus

Having a single focus is a powerful thing – it makes life simple and a goal achievable. All I needed to do each day was pedal. Yes, there were logistics to worry about, a camera crew to lead, and shots to direct, but they fed into the main objective, which was to head east.

Focus was also my saving grace. There were several occasions where I could have sustained injuries or real danger but my focus on the destination had me pedaling through and out of those situations.

For instance, cycling along major highways next to speeding vehicles. I witnessed more dead animals than live ones. I could have been a casualty myself.

At the final home stretch, with only 14 miles to go to Baltimore's Inner Harbor, Derek and I rode past upscale

Ellicott City, and very quickly after, found ourselves in the heart of sketchy neighborhoods with low-income housing projects. We were stared at and unwelcome in those areas. I understood then that ignorance is bliss – we didn't have foreknowledge of the area, rode right into it and got out unharmed.

Conflict

Four weeks after I got home, I asked for and received an estimate from Tom for editing the documentary. It wasn't until several weeks later that I finally received his quote. I was flabbergasted. It was twice as much as the verbal estimate he and Sam had given me during the trip.

I had underestimated the cost of producing a high-resolution, full-length film with original soundtrack and animation, color grading, and sound engineering.

I took the high quote and tardiness in response to be a sign of non-interest on their part to carry on working with me.

I was also broke, having had to dig into my savings to fund a large part of the trip.

So I searched for another video editor and found a freelancer who was also a semi-professional snowboarder. I thought, here's an experienced sports person and outdoorsmen, plus a filmmaker. Surely he would cut a good film.

I commissioned him to cut a one-minute trailer, liked his work, and was prepared to offer him the job of editing the full documentary for a fraction of Tom's quote. At the same time I came clean and informed Tom that I was about to commission someone else to edit the documentary.

Tom didn't take my message well. He viewed my action as an obvious breach of contract. Both he and Sam had taken on the assignment of filming the documentary with the view that they would eventually see the entire project to completion, including editing the documentary. I scoured through our written contract and found nothing that said they would be editing the documentary. A separate contract would have had to be drafted for that job. I felt like I had the right to select who I wanted to work with.

The correspondence that followed wasn't pretty. Tom and I were upset with each other for not upholding our ends of the agreement and our words showed it.

At the same time, the independent video editor was anxious to start editing the documentary. I informed him not to start work until I resolved a pressing, messy situation. He was agreeable.

IIIIIIIIIIIIIII

After several weeks of hostile written exchanges with Tom, I decided I needed to clear my head. I went out cycling. As I waited for the light to turn green at a traffic junction, I noticed a beat up car to my left. Its driver, a heavyset Mexican lady, was exchanging harsh remarks with her male passenger, presumably a lover or partner. I couldn't understand what they were saying, but could feel their angry vibes spilling out of the car through the open windows. Standing there on my bicycle, next to a verbally-violent couple sitting in a car, I decided that I didn't like to be in aggressive environments and that I had the power to resolve a situation tactfully. I decided to initiate a peace process with Tom.

I wrote him an email, describing what I had just witnessed (about the angry couple), apologized for my rude behavior, and indicated my interest to have him and Sam edit the documentary.

Tom responded with grace, we resolved our differences, and resumed our working relationship after signing a freshly drafted, mutually agreed upon written contract.

IIIIIIIIIIIIIII

Having contracted Sam and Tom to edit the documentary, I had to break the news to the other video editor.

A new conflict ensued. I was accused of going back on my word. He had accepted my offer to edit the documentary and now I had decided to pull the plug on him.

I was distraught. From one battle to another. More hostility followed between us. After several rounds of correspondence and months later, we finally resolved the situation.

Looking back, I was extremely inexperienced. I thought that my decade-long training as a paralegal would have given me sufficient knowledge to navigate contractual issues, but I was wrong.

I learned that words have consequences, especially in a contractual relationship where parties rely on both spoken and written words and are expected to honor their words. I learned from this experience to be careful not to over-promise what I can't deliver and to deliver on what I have already promised.

▲ A low moment in Kremmling, Colorado. The relentless mosquito attacks in Colorado and unforgiving winds in Kansas sent me on a downward spiral.

Closure

Finding My Identity

For a good nine months after I returned home, I was lost and confused. I didn't understand why I felt what I felt. I couldn't explain what was happening to myself.

I had completed an epic adventure. Why was I feeling so low? Was it post-adventure blues? You know, the kind you get after you return from a vacation. Or was it something deeper and more complex than that?

Over the years I've learned that the best way to introduce clarity into the mumble and jumble of our chaotic thoughts is to put them down in writing. Think of it as capturing a thousand fallen maple leaves and arranging them neatly in a scrap book so you can make notes on each leaf, its color and texture.

So I started writing how I felt.

I noticed that the things that used to be important to me weren't anymore.

I've always loved food and sought to satisfy each gastronomic craving I had. Now, food is simply a matter of function rather than enjoyment.

I've always liked people and noise. Now, I dislike noise and enjoy being alone. But nothing I wrote would help me understand what was happening to me.

One day, my friend, Theresa, gently said to me: "You don't always need to be spectacular, you know – you can afford to be ordinary sometimes."

I stopped in my tracks. Her words were simple but true. I had been trying to live up to my extraordinary ride across America. I was living in the cocoon of the bike ride, a past life, and refused to embrace the current, ordinary life. This disillusionment created a void in my heart so large that nothing I could possibly conjure up next could fill that vacuum.

It took a toll on my marriage as well. I had neglected my husband for a senseless pursuit of the outdoors and more epic journeys. I realized how terribly selfish I had been, while my husband had been incredibly supportive. It hit home that it was only right that I devote more time and attention to him.

If life was a cycle, then a spectacular wonder is often followed by things less than spectacular. Every mountaintop experience is met with steep descents and long walks through the valley, before approaching the next mountain pass.

Now that I had experienced the mountaintop thrill of cycling across America, my life back home is my walk through the valley until I get to the next mountaintop.

Remember, the next time you're down and out, when you're walking in the valley, keep walking. It's only temporary. You'll get out and up eventually.

Personal Closure

Never would I have thought that writing this book would bring me the healing I needed.

The bike ride caused a tremendous amount of pain to me physically, mentally, emotionally, and psychologically.

When Derek asked me if I would ride across America again, I replied with a firm "never" without thinking twice. But after spending a full year writing this book and drawing out the memories and emotions following the bike ride from June to July 2014, the states that tormented me the most with torrential rain, hail, snow, cold and unceasing wind, those are the very states that I would now like to return to and re-experience. It is almost as if I know they won't hurt me like they did the first time, and I'd like to return to take a chance at rebuilding a relationship that didn't start off on the right foot.

Derek

Derek moved home to Kansas after our bike ride, and continued cycling and exploring the flat plains of the windy state. He even taught spin classes for a short period. The women in class loved him. He eventually met a lovely lady and married her by Palos Verdes Beach in Los Angeles. I drove six hours south to be his official photographer, while my husband played the march-in song on his guitar. The happy couple now lives in Mesa, Arizona.

An introspective moment back home in California.

RECONCILIATION

Recently, I went home to Malaysia to visit my parents. Baring my heart, I told my dad how unhappy I was growing up, and how he caned me until I was 17. To my surprise, he didn't remember those brutal caning sessions or much of the pain he inflicted on me. He also didn't realize how his military-like parenting style made my siblings and me feel restrained and hurt most of the time.

Looking into his now old and worn eyes, I realized that it was useless to harbor anger and negative feelings towards him, because if I were to measure his actions objectively, he wasn't a mean man – he was simply doing the best he could. Together with my mom, they struggled to raise four young children with limited finances. When money ran low and frustration ran high, he ruled the household with a tight iron-fist. Being the youngest and most rebellious, I bore the brunt of his beatings.

I realized that we are products of our past, but we don't have to be prisoners of it. From a painful past, we learn to break free from limitations. From a happy past, we learn to build upon it. Either way, they aren't meant to hold us back; they are footholds for us to move forward in life.

Instead of being chained to the memories of the past, I resolve to re-create a new future with my dad. After all, it was his relentless emphasis on education and knowledge that made me who I am today – insatiably curious and doggedly determined to push boundaries. For that, I am extremely grateful.

Gratitude

What started out as a desire to travel the country on two wheels ultimately became a journey where I discovered strength from vulnerability and the power of community.

I learned that no success is a solo effort, and that I can do so much more when I am honest, transparent, reach out for help and trust that people are far more willing to help than I think they are.

Because I lacked experience in ultra distance cycling, filmmaking, and fund raising, I reached out to people for help, largely via email and social media. People who didn't have answers for me referred me to people who did.

Because I needed to ensure my safety in a foreign country and keep my sanity for long hours on the road, I found a reliable and witty buddy in Derek.

When the ride became an increasingly tough battle against time and weather, encouragement and prayers would pour in from people all over the world who were following my journey. I was surprised to find kind messages from supporters in Japan, Germany, Finland and even Kazakhstan.

My heart swells with gratitude whenever I look back at the summer of 2014. At no point throughout the entire trip did I accomplish anything on my own. I had an unfair advantage: an incredibly supportive team of family, friends, and strangers-turned-friends who rallied themselves around me so I could cycle across America and produce a film that documented the honest reality of the journey.

Documentary

"Hi my name is Angeline, I'm 35 years old, I've been an athlete all throughout my life and I love pizza."

That was the opening line of my debut documentary which took four months to edit.

Sam, Tom and I plotted out a story line or script, then they gathered all the footage recorded during the ride, which came up to hundreds of hours, picked out scenes that fit the script, and edited the film accordingly. We went through three rounds of editing before we were pleased with the result – a 39-minute documentary that detailed an ordinary girl's dream to cycle across America in under 40 days and the challenges that ensued.

The entire documentary edit process took place online. We relied heavily on email and occasionally, on Google Hangout.

On two accounts, that opening statement in the film is no longer relevant. I'm no longer 35, and while it's true that I love pizza, I hardly eat it these days. I have become more conscious of what I eat because food can either make me feel good or terrible, train and perform well or horribly. So I pick and choose my food more carefully these days. I hardly eat grains. They make me lethargic and make my stomach bloat. To make my life simple, I stopped eating pizza. Do I crave it? From time to time. But I don't crave for the taste of wheat or dough as much as the fragrance of something baked or toasted. So I can toast something else, fish, chicken, or even a slice of banana, and that will be enough.

It always makes me smile when my friends or people who have seen my documentary invite me for a meal and say,

"Let's have pizza!" because they recall that line from the film.

The beauty of a documentary is that it captures a real life story at a particular point of time – it is almost as if the audience is present at the same time, and not merely bystanders or spectators.

I had wanted to be honest about the journey of the ride, and present the full story including the triumphant and low moments. I think the film accomplished that.

llllllllllllll

When I looked through my footage and saw recordings of myself, I shuddered at what an arrogant and disrespectful person I was. It's been said that we are our worst critics. I certainly didn't like who and how I was. It also hit home how frequently I was on my phone, in the presence of other people. I have neglected tangible, human interaction for intangible social media interaction. I resolved to change after watching that footage. I reduced my phone usage in the company of friends and family and practiced extra courtesy to the people around me.

When the film was completed, I published it on YouTube. It's free for anybody to watch. I made it available for free because that was the motivation behind the film – to share a personal journey and to inspire others to pursue their dreams.

To date, the documentary has garnered over 50,000 views on YouTube. I have received many kind messages from people telling me how inspired they were and that they have either picked up a sport or started running or cycling because of my film.

Some have also been inspired to go on a journey that they have postponed for a long time due to lack of financial resources and fear of the unknown.

In order to spread the film more widely, I organized beer and pizza party screenings for friends and encouraged them to invite their friends. I also screened the film in schools, companies and banks. Every time I did, messages would pour in from the attendees telling me how inspired they were.

That positive encouragement has helped me stay on course even as I wonder sometimes if marketing the film is simply self-promotion. My close friends remind me that my story is an example of breaking personal limitations, and that is a powerful message that needs to reach more people.

And so I will keep spreading the message of pursuing your dreams through the film and this book that you now hold in your hands. It has been a fun journey and I can only thank every one of you for partnering me in this adventure, in one way or another.

||||||||||||||||

The documentary, Angie Across America,
is available on YouTube and on
www.angieacrossamerica.com

End of the ride at Inner ▶
Harbor, Baltimore.

"Don't ask what the world needs. Ask what makes you come alive, and go do it. Because what the world needs is people who have come alive."

– Howard Thurman, African American author, philosopher, and civil rights leader

Epilogue

We live among seven billion people, many of whom are survivors, but only a handful are dreamers and doers.

I am not content to be a mere survivor.

This is precisely why I decided to cycle across America. It wasn't just a selfish dream to see the country. It was a desire to have an extraordinary dream and go after it, come hell or high water.

It is not always necessary to do something monumental in order to find yourself, although it helps to make yourself so uncomfortable you have to do something you normally wouldn't do otherwise.

Everyone has a different journey in life. You don't have to cycle across America to discover yourself. Getting uncomfortable and out of your skin could mean leaving your current nine-to-five job and starting your own business. Or taking time off from work to care for an ailing parent. Or it might involve some element of travel – perhaps a three-month absence from work to travel to places you have never been in order to discover yourself.

Dreams are precious and happen for a specific purpose. If you conceive it in your mind, feel a tug in your heart and nurture it in your soul, then you should pursue it.

Don't simply brush it aside because the dream is too huge or beyond you at the present moment. That dream was formed in you for a special reason.

We are unique and our journeys will take on different forms.

I know riding across America in 39 days is not for everyone – it was an adventure that was uniquely mine, one which played an instrumental role in helping me reach into the deep crevices of my soul to uncover my past memories, hurt, pain and lessons that made me who I am today. My tough upbringing served as a strong foundation upon which I built a resilient spirit to weather any storm that comes my way.

Sometimes in the pursuit of your dreams you might ask: "Is what I'm doing epic enough? Will it inspire people to pursue their dreams?"

Those were the questions I asked myself when I decided to cycle across America.

Be very confident of who you are and all that you do. You have to live true to your personal calling. Do not let doubt or critics rob you of your voice. Do not let the next record-breaking attempt and amazing feats of high achievers distract or derail you from your unique purpose.

Can you imagine a world where everyone is true to his or her own voice? We would do, create, and accomplish the most amazing things on earth.

Go on. *Just Do It*.

Acknowledgments

Even as I write these acknowledgments, I noticed a common thread: I thank these precious ones for fighting the demons in my mind concerning my ability and craft, an area I struggle with compulsively throughout my life (I suspect many creatives are in the same shoes but I have a slight advantage – I have these amazing individuals who helped me up my game when I wanted to pull out).

||||||||||||||||

My family for being extremely patient and understanding despite not fully understanding why I do the things I do – pushing myself beyond my physical and emotional limits just so I can live out a dream, and hopefully, in the process, inspire someone else through my journey. Their acceptance of my self identity found in ultra endurance sports is important for me to keep pursuing it in full confidence. Thank you especially to my mom, sister, and my parents in law – all of whom love me very much and made sure I know that.

My closest friends including Grace Wong and Bevan Foo, who don't share my passion in sports but never fail to encourage me through my down times and for believing in my ability to weather through any challenges thrown my way in the pursuit of any audacious adventure I embark on.

Pastor Adam and Keira Smallcombe – if I lived in their home and minds, I would believe myself to be invincible and capable of greater feats than I ever think possible – and why shouldn't that be the case? Their incredible love and unceasing faith in each other, God and people is the catalyst that propels me forward.

Coach Colin for singlehandedly transforming the amateur cyclist in me into one who rides 100, 150 miles a day with ease, in a matter of months. He is the most patient and gracious man I know (though I've never met him in person) – there were countless times where I doubted myself but Colin knew exactly what to say to spur and lift me out of the pit. He made me realize that above and beyond physical preparation is a coach who helps you prepare mentally and emotionally. Colin did just that, without which I would not have the fortitude to complete the ride at all.

Coach Victor for teaching me to break hurdles in my mind concerning the value and contribution I have to offer to the world through my documentary, book and talks. He was instrumental in helping me close the gaps in my writing roadblocks and urging me to put my work out to the world when I wanted to shrink back and hide.

Paul Bragiel for demonstrating by example that it is possible to overcome the odds and take steps towards realizing a childhood dream of competing in the Olympic Games. His unlikely story from a regular over-weight guy to a cross-country skier inspired me to throw aside my doubts and ride across America, a dream that was huge and impossible in my mind at that point in time.

Seth Godin for encouraging me to trust my work and put this book out because I need no other approval to be uniquely me.

Derek Sivers for constantly thinking out of the box and helping me to do likewise, especially with the publication of this book and the efforts to have this book reach as many people as possible.

My editor, Margaret Crandall for burning numerous weekends reading my drafts and editing them. She was meticulous and insightful. She helped hone me into a better writer with each draft. She is amazing beyond the call of duty and if I praised her any more, she'd think I'm buttering her up. I'm not – I like her to bits because she is utterly candid, honest, and witty, and she gives so much.

Theresa Tan – I have the honor of calling her my friend, mentor, advisor, consultant, and impromptu editor. She stepped into my world and I can't imagine not having known a more wonderful person as she. Her ability to be entirely true to herself and letting her colors shine is so infectious, just the thought of her cheers me so. Yes, she is that special.

And finally, my husband. Three times during my six-week adventure, my husband Jason woke up at 3.00 a.m. on a Saturday, got on a five-hour plane ride, and drove a rental car six hours east to an obscure, tiny town in the middle of America, saw me for half a day, and turned around to get home by Sunday night.

The operation was logistically challenging, financially

demanding, and physically draining. His destination was never certain until the very last hour because I was a moving target. I cycled with a GPS tracker which beamed my exact location every three minutes to the web. He'd monitor a little blue dot moving at snail speed across the computer screen, pick the city he'd fly to, and purchase a last-minute plane ticket. Even as he arrived at the airport and planned his driving route to meet me, it was still a mystery where exactly I'd stop for the night.

"Why didn't he just travel with you for the entire six weeks?" people asked. Well, someone had to bring home a regular income. Jason had to work to finance us both and couldn't take six weeks of unpaid leave to accompany a sojourning spouse, yet knew how much it meant to me to have him near for moral support, so he took it upon himself to travel the distance and burn a big hole in his wallet for last-minute plane tickets.

During each short visit and the little precious time we had together, I'd recount my stories of misery to him and as I did, cry and beg him to stay longer. He'd hug me, tell me I must be strong and that he couldn't stay longer because we each had our destination to go to – him, to work; me, to pedal east. In hindsight, gosh, I must have acted like a drama queen, but trust me, when you're doing something so far out of your comfort zone, you realize how wonderful it is to have your best friend near.

It amazes me how incredibly trusting and respectful my husband is of my dreams and activities. I am constantly engaged in sports where I spend half my time with men. There are usually three times as many men as women on every bike ride or group run. For my ride across America, I spent 39 full days in the company of a man I didn't know beforehand. Derek Wilson would turn out to be the best riding buddy I could possibly ask for. He made the hours and days go by quickly with his incredible sense of humor and he taught me to appreciate life with his easy-going attitude.

IIIIIIIIIIIIIII

I am beyond thankful for all of these dear ones, and for everyone else whom I have not specifically mentioned here. Your impact in my life travels beyond me – it is also reaching other people, in a positive manner, through this book.

About The Author

Angeline Tan is an adventurer, writer, filmmaker and
motivational speaker with a special interest in inspiring
change. She started writing at age five, having been greatly
inspired by Enid Blyton, a best-selling English author of
children's books. *Crazy Cycling Chick* is her debut book. She
is the creator of an independently produced documentary,
Angie Across America, which covers the journey in this book.
She lives in the San Francisco Bay Area.

www.angieacrossamerica.com